Christian Ethics: A Very Short Introduction

VERY SHORT INTRODUCTIONS are for anyone wanting a stimulating and accessible way into a new subject. They are written by experts, and have been translated into more than 45 different languages.

The series began in 1995, and now covers a wide variety of topics in every discipline. The VSI library now contains over 500 volumes—a Very Short Introduction to everything from Psychology and Philosophy of Science to American History and Relativity—and continues to grow in every subject area.

Titles in the series include the following:

AFRICAN HISTORY John Parker and
    Richard Rathbone
AGEING Nancy A. Pachana
ALGEBRA Peter M. Higgins
AMERICAN HISTORY Paul S. Boyer
AMERICAN IMMIGRATION
    David A. Gerber
AMERICAN LEGAL HISTORY
    G. Edward White
AMERICAN POLITICAL HISTORY
    Donald Critchlow
AMERICAN POLITICAL PARTIES
    AND ELECTIONS L. Sandy Maisel
AMERICAN POLITICS
    Richard M. Valelly
THE AMERICAN PRESIDENCY
    Charles O. Jones
AMERICAN SLAVERY
    Heather Andrea Williams
ANARCHISM Colin Ward
ANCIENT EGYPT Ian Shaw
ANCIENT GREECE Paul Cartledge
THE ANCIENT NEAR EAST
    Amanda H. Podany
ANCIENT PHILOSOPHY Julia Annas
ANCIENT WARFARE Harry Sidebottom
ANGLICANISM Mark Chapman
THE ANGLO-SAXON AGE John Blair
ANIMAL BEHAVIOUR
    Tristram D. Wyatt
ANIMAL RIGHTS David DeGrazia
ANXIETY Daniel Freeman and
    Jason Freeman
ARCHAEOLOGY Paul Bahn

ARISTOTLE Jonathan Barnes
ART HISTORY Dana Arnold
ART THEORY Cynthia Freeland
ASTROPHYSICS James Binney
ATHEISM Julian Baggini
THE ATMOSPHERE Paul I. Palmer
AUGUSTINE Henry Chadwick
BACTERIA Sebastian G. B. Amyes
BARTHES Jonathan Culler
BEAUTY Roger Scruton
THE BIBLE John Riches
BLACK HOLES Katherine Blundell
BLOOD Chris Cooper
THE BRAIN Michael O'Shea
THE BRICS Andrew F. Cooper
BRITISH POLITICS Anthony Wright
BUDDHA Michael Carrithers
BUDDHISM Damien Keown
BUDDHIST ETHICS Damien Keown
BYZANTIUM Peter Sarris
CANCER Nicholas James
CAPITALISM James Fulcher
CATHOLICISM Gerald O'Collins
THE CELTS Barry Cunliffe
CHEMISTRY Peter Atkins
CHOICE THEORY Michael Allingham
CHRISTIANITY Linda Woodhead
CIRCADIAN RHYTHMS Russell Foster
    and Leon Kreitzman
CITIZENSHIP Richard Bellamy
CLASSICAL MYTHOLOGY
    Helen Morales
CLASSICS Mary Beard and
    John Henderson

CLIMATE Mark Maslin
CLIMATE CHANGE Mark Maslin
THE COLD WAR Robert McMahon
COMBINATORICS Robin Wilson
COMMUNISM Leslie Holmes
COMPUTER SCIENCE Subrata Dasgupta
CONSCIOUSNESS Susan Blackmore
CONTEMPORARY ART
    Julian Stallabrass
CORAL REEFS Charles Sheppard
COSMOLOGY Peter Coles
THE CRUSADES Christopher Tyerman
DADA AND SURREALISM
    David Hopkins
DANTE Peter Hainsworth and
    David Robey
DARWIN Jonathan Howard
THE DEAD SEA SCROLLS
    Timothy Lim
DECOLONIZATION Dane Kennedy
DEMOCRACY Bernard Crick
DESIGN John Heskett
DINOSAURS David Norman
DREAMING J. Allan Hobson
DRUGS Les Iversen
DRUIDS Barry Cunliffe
THE EARTH Martin Redfern
ECONOMICS Partha Dasgupta
EGYPTIAN MYTH Geraldine Pinch
THE ELEMENTS Philip Ball
EMOTION Dylan Evans
EMPIRE Stephen Howe
ENGLISH LITERATURE Jonathan Bate
THE ENLIGHTENMENT
    John Robertson
EPICUREANISM Catherine Wilson
EPIDEMIOLOGY Rodolfo Saracci
ETHICS Simon Blackburn
EUGENICS Philippa Levine
THE EUROPEAN UNION John Pinder
    and Simon Usherwood
EVOLUTION Brian and
    Deborah Charlesworth
EXISTENTIALISM Thomas Flynn
FASCISM Kevin Passmore
FEMINISM Margaret Walters
THE FIRST WORLD WAR
    Michael Howard
FORENSIC PSYCHOLOGY
    David Canter
FOUCAULT Gary Gutting
FREE SPEECH Nigel Warburton
FREE WILL Thomas Pink
FREUD Anthony Storr
FUNDAMENTALISM Malise Ruthven
FUNGI Nicholas P. Money
GALAXIES John Gribbin
GALILEO Stillman Drake
GAME THEORY Ken Binmore
GANDHI Bhikhu Parekh
GEOGRAPHY John Matthews and
    David Herbert
GEOPOLITICS Klaus Dodds
GLOBAL CATASTROPHES Bill McGuire
GLOBAL ECONOMIC HISTORY
    Robert C. Allen
GLOBALIZATION Manfred Steger
GOD John Bowker
HABERMAS James Gordon Finlayson
HEGEL Peter Singer
HINDUISM Kim Knott
HISTORY John H. Arnold
THE HISTORY OF LIFE Michael Benton
THE HISTORY OF MATHEMATICS
    Jacqueline Stedall
THE HISTORY OF MEDICINE
    William Bynum
THE HISTORY OF TIME
    Leofranc Holford-Strevens
HIV AND AIDS Alan Whiteside
HOLLYWOOD Peter Decherney
HUMAN ANATOMY
    Leslie Klenerman
HUMAN EVOLUTION Bernard Wood
HUMAN RIGHTS Andrew Clapham
IDEOLOGY Michael Freeden
INDIAN PHILOSOPHY Sue Hamilton
INFINITY Ian Stewart
INFORMATION Luciano Floridi
INNOVATION Mark Dodgson and
    David Gann
INTELLIGENCE Ian J. Deary
INTERNATIONAL
    MIGRATION Khalid Koser
INTERNATIONAL RELATIONS
    Paul Wilkinson
ISLAM Malise Ruthven
ISLAMIC HISTORY Adam Silverstein
JESUS Richard Bauckham
JOURNALISM Ian Hargreaves

JUDAISM Norman Solomon
JUNG Anthony Stevens
KABBALAH Joseph Dan
KANT Roger Scruton
KNOWLEDGE Jennifer Nagel
THE KORAN Michael Cook
LATE ANTIQUITY Gillian Clark
LAW Raymond Wacks
THE LAWS OF THERMODYNAMICS
    Peter Atkins
LEADERSHIP Keith Grint
LEARNING Mark Haselgrove
LIGHT Ian Walmsley
LINGUISTICS Peter Matthews
LITERARY THEORY Jonathan Culler
LOCKE John Dunn
LOGIC Graham Priest
MACHIAVELLI Quentin Skinner
MARTIN LUTHER Scott H. Hendrix
MARTYRDOM Jolyon Mitchell
MARX Peter Singer
MATHEMATICS Timothy Gowers
THE MEANING OF LIFE Terry Eagleton
MEASUREMENT David Hand
MEDICAL ETHICS Tony Hope
MEDIEVAL BRITAIN John Gillingham
    and Ralph A. Griffiths
MEDIEVAL LITERATURE
    Elaine Treharne
MEDIEVAL PHILOSOPHY
    John Marenbon
MEMORY Jonathan K. Foster
METAPHYSICS Stephen Mumford
MICROSCOPY Terence Allen
MILITARY JUSTICE Eugene R. Fidell
MODERN ART David Cottington
MODERN CHINA Rana Mitter
MODERN IRELAND Senia Pašeta
MODERN ITALY Anna Cento Bull
MODERN JAPAN
    Christopher Goto-Jones
MODERNISM Christopher Butler
MOLECULAR BIOLOGY Aysha Divan
    and Janice A. Royds
MOLECULES Philip Ball
MOONS David A. Rothery
MUSIC Nicholas Cook
MYTH Robert A. Segal
NEOLIBERALISM Manfred Steger and
    Ravi Roy

NEWTON Robert Iliffe
NIETZSCHE Michael Tanner
NORTH AMERICAN INDIANS
    Theda Perdue and Michael D. Green
NORTHERN IRELAND
    Marc Mulholland
NOTHING Frank Close
NUCLEAR PHYSICS Frank Close
NUTRITION David A. Bender
THE PALESTINIAN-ISRAELI
    CONFLICT Martin Bunton
PANDEMICS Christian W. McMillen
PARTICLE PHYSICS Frank Close
THE PERIODIC TABLE Eric R. Scerri
PHILOSOPHY Edward Craig
PHILOSOPHY IN THE ISLAMIC
    WORLD Peter Adamson
PHILOSOPHY OF LAW
    Raymond Wacks
PHILOSOPHY OF SCIENCE
    Samir Okasha
PHOTOGRAPHY Steve Edwards
PHYSICAL CHEMISTRY Peter Atkins
PLANETS David A. Rothery
PLATO Julia Annas
POLITICAL PHILOSOPHY David Miller
POLITICS Kenneth Minogue
POPULISM Cas Mudde and
    Cristóbal Rovira Kaltwasser
POSTCOLONIALISM Robert Young
POSTMODERNISM Christopher Butler
POSTSTRUCTURALISM
    Catherine Belsey
PREHISTORY Chris Gosden
PRESOCRATIC PHILOSOPHY
    Catherine Osborne
PSYCHIATRY Tom Burns
PSYCHOLOGY Gillian Butler and
    Freda McManus
PSYCHOTHERAPY Tom Burns and
    Eva Burns-Lundgren
PUBLIC HEALTH Virginia Berridge
QUANTUM THEORY
    John Polkinghorne
RACISM Ali Rattansi
THE REFORMATION Peter Marshall
RELATIVITY Russell Stannard
THE RENAISSANCE Jerry Brotton
RENAISSANCE ART
    Geraldine A. Johnson

REVOLUTIONS Jack A. Goldstone
RHETORIC Richard Toye
RISK Baruch Fischhoff and John Kadvany
RITUAL Barry Stephenson
RIVERS Nick Middleton
ROBOTICS Alan Winfield
ROMAN BRITAIN Peter Salway
THE ROMAN EMPIRE
    Christopher Kelly
THE ROMAN REPUBLIC
    David M. Gwynn
RUSSIAN HISTORY Geoffrey Hosking
THE RUSSIAN REVOLUTION
    S. A. Smith
SCHIZOPHRENIA Chris Frith and
    Eve Johnstone
SCIENCE AND RELIGION
    Thomas Dixon
SEXUALITY Véronique Mottier
SHAKESPEARE'S COMEDIES
    Bart van Es
SIKHISM Eleanor Nesbitt
SLEEP Steven W. Lockley and
    Russell G. Foster
SOCIAL AND CULTURAL
    ANTHROPOLOGY
    John Monaghan and Peter Just
SOCIAL PSYCHOLOGY Richard J. Crisp
SOCIAL WORK Sally Holland and
    Jonathan Scourfield
SOCIALISM Michael Newman
SOCIOLOGY Steve Bruce

SOCRATES C. C. W. Taylor
SOUND Mike Goldsmith
THE SOVIET UNION Stephen Lovell
THE SPANISH CIVIL WAR
    Helen Graham
SPANISH LITERATURE Jo Labanyi
STATISTICS David J. Hand
STUART BRITAIN John Morrill
SYMMETRY Ian Stewart
TAXATION Stephen Smith
TELESCOPES Geoff Cottrell
TERRORISM Charles Townshend
THEOLOGY David F. Ford
TIBETAN BUDDHISM
    Matthew T. Kapstein
THE TROJAN WAR Eric H. Cline
THE TUDORS John Guy
THE UNITED NATIONS
    Jussi M. Hanhimäki
THE U.S. CONGRESS Donald A. Ritchie
THE U.S. SUPREME COURT
    Linda Greenhouse
THE VIKINGS Julian Richards
VIRUSES Dorothy H. Crawford
WAR AND TECHNOLOGY
    Alex Roland
WILLIAM SHAKESPEARE
    Stanley Wells
WITCHCRAFT Malcolm Gaskill
THE WORLD TRADE
    ORGANIZATION Amrita Narlikar
WORLD WAR II Gerhard L. Weinberg

D. Stephen Long

CHRISTIAN ETHICS

A Very Short Introduction

OXFORD
UNIVERSITY PRESS

OXFORD
UNIVERSITY PRESS

Great Clarendon Street, Oxford ox2 6DP

Oxford University Press is a department of the University of Oxford.
It furthers the University's objective of excellence in research, scholarship,
and education by publishing worldwide in

Oxford New York

Auckland Cape Town Dar es Salaam Hong Kong Karachi
Kuala Lumpur Madrid Melbourne Mexico City Nairobi
New Delhi Shanghai Taipei Toronto

With offices in

Argentina Austria Brazil Chile Czech Republic France Greece
Guatemala Hungary Italy Japan Poland Portugal Singapore
South Korea Switzerland Thailand Turkey Ukraine Vietnam

Oxford is a registered trade mark of Oxford University Press
in the UK and in certain other countries

Published in the United States
by Oxford University Press Inc., New York

British Library Cataloguing in Publication Data

Data available

Library of Congress Cataloging in Publication Data

Data available

Typeset by SPI Publisher Services, Pondicherry, India
Printed and bound by
CPI Group (UK) Ltd, Croydon, CR0 4YY

ISBN 978-0-19-956886-4

For the people and staff of Evanston First United Methodist Church.

Contents

List of illustrations xiii

Introduction 1

1 The sources of Christian ethics 13

2 The history of Christian ethics 51

3 Christian ethics in and beyond modernity 80

4 Sex, money, and power: some questions for Christian ethics 106

References 123

Further reading 129

Index 133

List of illustrations

1 Reredos at First United Methodist Church, Evanston, Illinois **5**

© 2008 S. Smith Photography (<http://www.ssmithphotos.com>)

2 Raphael's *School of Athens* **14**

Vatican Museums and Galleries. Photo: © 2010 Scala, Florence

3 *The Triumph of St Thomas Aquinas* **22**

Santa Maria Novella, Florence. Photo: © 2010 Scala, Florence/Fondo Edifici di Culto, Min. dell'Interno

4 Edward Hick's *Peaceable Kingdom* **26**

Worcester Art Museum, Massachusetts. Photo: © The Bridgeman Art Library

5 The Ark of the Covenant **39**

© Hulton Archive/Getty Images

6 Jastrow's duck-rabbit **49**

7 Papal insignia **69**

© Rmherman

8 Saint Ambrose confronting the emperor Theodosius **75**

The National Gallery, London. Photo: © 2010 Scala, Florence

9 Diego Rivera's mural showing Bartolomé de las Casas **85**

Museum of the Palace of Fine Arts, Mexico. © 2010 Banco de México Diego Rivera Frida Kahlo Museums Trust, Mexico, D.F./DACS. Photo: © 2010 Art Resource/Scala, Florence

10 Grünewald's crucifixion from the Isenheim altar **103**

Unterlinden Museum, Colmar. © Erich Lessing/akg-images

Introduction

To bring the terms 'Christian' and 'ethics' together and treat them as referring to a common subject matter might strike persons of faith or those without it as odd, perhaps even as a contradiction. For some modern persons, the term 'Christian' conjures up images of past immoral activities: crusades, the Inquisition, the conquest of the Americas, religious wars, the Galileo affair, defences of slavery and patriarchy. To qualify 'ethics' by 'Christian' would regress to a time before the considerable gains of living well that we moderns have accomplished. 'Ethics' liberates us from harmful Christian practices. It holds Christianity accountable for its past and present failures, even to the point of judging it as evil. Take, for instance, the charges Christopher Hitchens brings against all organized religion, including Christianity:

> Violent, irrational, intolerant, allied to racism and tribalism and bigotry, invested in ignorance and hostile to free inquiry, contemptuous of women and coercive toward children; organized religion ought to have a great deal on its conscience. There is one more charge to be added to the bill of indictment. With a necessary part of its collective mind, religion looks forward to the destruction of the world.

If Hitchens is correct, then 'ethics' cannot be allied with Christianity; it is its alternative. A sensitive ethical conscience would abandon Christian faith.

Yet those who reject faith are not the only ones who find the juxtaposition of the terms 'Christian' and 'ethics' troubling, albeit for very different reasons. 'Ethics' is most often understood as a thoroughly human endeavour. We are ethical through our own resources. One of the greatest ethicists who ever lived, Aristotle, taught this. For him, every thing has a natural end to which it is directed. For instance, the end of an acorn is to be an oak tree. Intrinsic to an acorn's nature are the means to achieve this end. With the right nurturing, proper soil, light, nutrients, and so on, the acorn will naturally achieve its end. Likewise, the human creature has a natural, ethical end, which is to live a good life that achieves happiness, or what in Greek is called *eudaimonia*. We have everything in our nature that we need for such an end if it flourishes in the proper circumstances.

Not only Aristotle but also much of modern ethics assumes the autonomy of human nature as the basis for ethics. But for Christians, to think that we can achieve the good through our own resources is the heresy known as 'Pelagianism'. It denies that we need grace and/or supernatural virtues in order to achieve our end, which is to dwell with God and have God dwell with us. Such an end – friendship with God – exceeds any natural ability we bring about on our own. Therefore, while the Christian faith agrees with Aristotle that we have a good end for which we were made, it denies that we naturally possess all that we need to achieve it. We need something more – 'grace', otherwise known as the gift of the Holy Spirit – in order to reach this good end. It is beyond, or more than, natural, which the term 'super-natural' suggests.

So here we have two very different objections to relating the terms 'Christian' and 'ethics', one that seeks to preserve ethics from Christianity, the other preserving Christianity from ethics. Given these concerns, is it possible to bring 'Christian' and 'ethics' together into a coherent subject matter?

Why Christianity does and does not need ethics

Both the historical practice of Christianity and its own doctrines require a Christian assessment of ethics and an ethical assessment of Christianity. Christianity may be more, but it should never be less, than ethical. Sometimes the beauty of non-Christian ethics compels Christianity to be accountable to that ethics. Sometimes the reduction of Christianity to ethics requires it to insist that it is more than ethics. Even the term 'super-natural' assumes a role for the natural. Although Christianity never assumes we can finally redeem ourselves, the more (super-) that is given to the 'natural' presumes a role for 'nature' in redemption.

The common Catholic expression 'grace presupposes and perfects nature' captures this insight well. Not all forms of Christianity are pleased with this expression. As we will see, the Reformed theologian Karl Barth suspected it might bring too much 'pagan' morality into Christianity. It might allow for a 'natural law' approach to ethics that eschews grace. But even he recognized the importance of developing a 'Christian ethics'. These two terms have been associated throughout the history of the Christian Church in varying ways by its diverse traditions, Catholic, Orthodox, and Protestant. We will examine that variety below. However, at its best 'Christian ethics' allows both for the faith to illumine ethics and for a reasonable understanding of ethics to clarify the faith. But this is no easy task, for neither 'Christian' nor 'ethics' identifies a single, coherent subject matter upon which all could agree. If Christian faith is to provide insight into the strengths and limitations of the human pursuit of the good (ethics), and ethics is to help us clarify Christian faith, then we will need some understanding as to what these terms refer to before bringing them together.

What is 'Christian'?

This is no easy question to answer. The Christian Churches themselves do not offer a common, united answer. The Orthodox, Roman Catholics, Anglicans, Anabaptists, and Protestants both agree and disagree as to what it means to be 'Christian'. We also have divisions within these Churches. We have charismatics, evangelicals, progressives, revisionists, traditionalists, and the list goes on. Any single account of what the term 'Christian' means will leave some unsatisfied. This does not, of course, mean that anything passes as Christian. We can set forth some basic, foundational claims. For instance, at its core, Christians worship Jesus as God. This can be found in the architecture of any church. Whether it is a simple Protestant building or an ornate Catholic or Orthodox one, the very structure of churches centres on the worship of Jesus. 'Low' forms of worship, where perhaps the Bible is all that is found at the centre of the church, attest to this. Here the words of Jesus will be honoured and read, and prayers will be offered to him and in his name. Likewise, 'high' forms of worship, where the centre of worship might be an altar table on which a priest performs an elaborate ritual claiming that in the bread and wine Jesus is fully present, also attest to it. Priests, pastors, and laypersons say things on these occasions such as 'the Word of the Lord' after reading Holy Scripture or 'the Body of Christ' after the prayer for Holy Communion. This is a rather remarkable practice, for it suggests that the human being Jesus of Nazareth, who was crucified, died, and was buried, is still present. Christians then bend the knee to him, a sign of worship and adoration.

Take, for instance, the reredos shown in Illustration 1, a detailed wood screen standing in the sanctuary that was built for the 1948 World Council of Churches held at First United Methodist Church in Evanston, Illinois. When worshippers enter the church, this image greets them. A cross sits on an altar table and behind it is this reredos, a carving that depicts Jesus's birth, crucifixion,

4

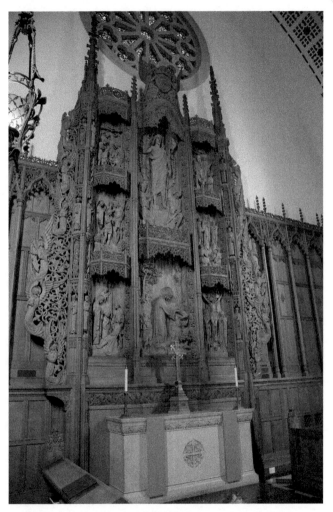

1. Reredos at First United Methodist Church, Evanston, Illinois. The life of Jesus is depicted and made the centre of worship

resurrection, and ascension. This forms the centre of Christian worship. All persons entering the building are directed towards him.

Yet Christians also worship Jesus within the context of a shared understanding with Judaism as to who God is, for Christians share Scriptures with Jews and believe we cannot know God's identity without these shared Scriptures. Christians and Jews agree, for instance, that the Ten Commandments should be kept, that God is one, and that nothing but God deserves our worship. These basic rules are found in the first three Commandments given to Moses.

1. 'I am the Lord your God who brought you out of the land of Egypt. You shall have no other gods before me.'
2. 'You shall not make for yourself an idol, whether in the form of anything that is in heaven above or that is on the earth beneath, or that is in the water under the earth.'
3. 'You shall not make wrongful use of the name of the Lord your God, for the Lord will not acquit anyone who misuses his name.'

(Exodus 21:1–7, New Revised Standard Version)

These three commandments are at the heart of a proper Jewish and Christian recognition of God. God alone is to be worshipped, and no creature is to stand in God's place. Nor are we to use God's name for vain and empty things. Christians affirm these commandments, and nevertheless recognize that Jesus is a creature. How then can he be worshipped? Why are the images present in the reredos, as well as those in nearly every Christian church, not 'graven images' that violate the Second Commandment?

To answer this question requires a brief discussion of two central teachings upon which the viability of Christianity depends: that God is Triune and that Jesus is the Incarnation of God, one Person who is truly human and divine.

God is Triune

Christians worship Jesus as God, recognize he is fully human, and confess that humanity is not divinity. This worship must be done with care, for to worship humanity would be to worship an idol and violate the first two Commandments. The Christian teaching on the Trinity is necessary for this reason. It helps explain why Christians confess with Israel that God is one and at the same time include Jesus in the divine identity and worship him as well. This practice happened early in the Christian Church when the first believers sang hymns and offered prayers to Jesus, prophesied in his name, and made 'ritual use' of his name in baptisms and exorcism. They also confessed him before others and celebrated his presence in the Lord's Supper (or Eucharist). Jesus was understood to be divine, but he was neither a second god nor an intermediary divine figure between the real God and creation. The first Christians were Jews and so they could not have allowed for either of these possibilities in their worship practices. There was only one God.

After many years of reflection upon these basic practices, the bishops of the Church met in Councils at Constantinople and Nicaea (AD 325–81) and developed language to explain how God is one and at the same time three Persons, in as much as this can be explained. These Councils stated that God is one essence, but this one essence is found in three Persons: the Father, the Son, and the Holy Spirit. Each of these Persons is also the full essence of God. Each is regularly invoked in Christian worship as worthy of adoration. Each is considered to be an agent who made possible creation and redemption. The doctrine of the Trinity is not a mathematical computation. It says the Father is the essence of God (not one-third of God), as are the Son and the Holy Spirit, and all three Persons together are the one essence as well. Nonetheless, God does not have four essences, only one. Each Person is distinct from the others, yet they are one in essence.

The Incarnation

The doctrine of the Trinity sets forth the Christian conviction that Jesus can be worshipped along with the Father and the Spirit because each is necessary for the identity of the one God. Jesus is the Second Person of the Trinity, who is eternally begotten from the Father as the Word, or Logos, through whom all things are then made. This defines theology proper – the understanding of who God is. But it does not yet define God's actions on behalf of creatures. The doctrine of the Incarnation explains this. It states that the Second Person of the Trinity became fully human as Jesus of Nazareth at a specific time and place. The Incarnation is God's mission to restore a broken creation. It is not only the moment of Jesus's birth, but also the example of his life, his teachings, cross, resurrection, and ascension. All of this is important for how God redeems the creation. In Jesus, the Second Person of the Trinity gives himself over, not only to be born, but also to grow, develop, teach, be crucified and buried. Because of his obedience, God raised him from the dead and sets him as Ruler and Lord over all creation.

The Incarnation received its definitive form at the Council of Chalcedon in AD 451 in the 'Chalcedonian definition'. It confesses that Jesus is both fully human and fully God. Jesus was:

> born of the Virgin Mary, the Mother of God, according to the Manhood; one and the same Christ, Son, Lord, only begotten, to be acknowledged in two natures, inconfusedly, unchangeably, indivisibly, inseparably; the distinction of natures being by no means taken away by the union, but rather the property of each nature being preserved, and concurring in one Person and one Subsistence, not parted or divided into two persons, but one and the same Son, and only begotten, God the Word, the Lord Jesus Christ.

In other words, in the One Person Jesus of Nazareth, God and humanity are both present, but they are present in such a way that both remain what they are. One is not changed into another. God does not become human in some mythological sense. Nor does humanity cease being humanity. Yet they are now united. This unity is eternal, for Jesus's life, death, resurrection, and exaltation established the perfect intimacy between God and humanity.

This act of unification is central to Christianity, and to its particular understanding of ethics. As many of the church fathers put it, 'God became human so that humans can become god'. This does not confuse the divine and human nature, for in becoming 'god', creatures do not become 'God'. Instead, they become 'partakers of the divine nature' (2 Peter 1:4). This redeems creatures from sin, evil, and death, and is something they cannot do by themselves. It is why Christianity is more than natural; for this is something Jesus alone accomplished as the perfect union of God and humanity. He was crucified and raised from the dead, uniting creaturely reality to God. He now invites creatures to participate in that union by being reconciled with God and one another. Here is one important reason why ethics matters for Christianity; such reconciliation will have salutary consequences that should be identifiable in everyday life. For instance, the church father Athanasius, who was largely responsible for the language used for the teaching that God is Triune, wrote a small treatise on the Incarnation in which he suggested that the 'proof' of Christ's divinity is found in the new way of life it produces. He wrote:

> While they were yet idolaters, the Greeks and Barbarians were always at war with each other, and were even cruel to their own kith and kin.... Indeed the whole course of their life was carried on with weapons, and the sword with them replaced the staff and was the mainstay of all aid. All this time, as I said before, they were serving idols and offering sacrifices to demons, and for all the superstitious awe that accompanied this idol worship, nothing could wean them from that warlike spirit. But strange to relate, since they came over

to the school of Christ, as men moved with real compunction they have laid aside their murderous cruelty and are war-minded no more. On the contrary, all is peace among them and nothing remains save desire for friendship.

Athanasius probably wrote this before he himself was involved in many political contests and confrontations over the truth of Christian teaching and was subsequently exiled many times, as were his opponents. It is difficult to read the history of his life and that of the church of his day, or any day, and say, 'all is peace among them and nothing remains save desire for friendship'. Yet Athanasius gives witness to an important connection between Christianity and ethics. If God has reconciled humanity in a remarkable union between divinity and humanity, then we should expect to see the consequences of such an event.

Ethics: the Incarnation and election

But what kind of ethical event is such an act of reconciliation? Is it moral for God to elect one person from all the peoples and nations of the world and be exclusively united to this one person? Is it moral for God to choose one nation out of all the nations as God's elect people, and be incarnate in an individual from that nation? Several modern theologians do not think it is. For this reason, they raise moral objections to the doctrine of the Incarnation. For instance, in a 1977 book, *The Myth of God Incarnate*, John Hick and others suggested it was time Christians abandon the traditional teaching on the Incarnation and begin to see it as a myth. Hick stated:

> The writers of this book are convinced that another major theological development is called for in this last part of the twentieth century. The need arises from growing knowledge of Christian origins and involves a recognition that Jesus was (as he is presented in Acts 2:21) 'a man approved by God' for a special role within the divine purpose, and that the later conception of him as God

incarnate, the Second Person of the Holy Trinity living a human life is a mythological or poetic way of expressing his significance for us. This recognition is called for in the interests of truth; but it also has increasingly important practical implications for our relationship to the peoples of the other great world religions.

The 'growing knowledge of Christian origins' did not produce the results Hick and his co-authors imagined. Few scholars still claim that we can find mythological sources that directly led to the Christian doctrine of the Incarnation. But Hick's ethical claim still has a tremendous hold on our modern imagination. If divinity and humanity are united in Jesus in a way that they cannot be found at any other place, what does that say about Christian attitudes toward the 'other great world religions'? Will it not produce an immoral intolerance? If we lessen the unique claims Christians make about Jesus, then we can expand the doctrine of the Incarnation such that it includes all religions, and possibly even the world. Sallie McFague makes just this claim for a revised teaching on the Incarnation. She states that theology now needs to 'relativize the incarnation in relation to Jesus of Nazareth' and 'maximize' the relation of divinity to the 'cosmos', so that Jesus is 'paradigmatic of what we find everywhere; everything that is is the sacrament of God (the universe as God's body), but here and there we find that presence erupting in special ways'. Like Hick, this takes away any exclusive uniqueness to Christianity that would set it against other religions.

Hick and McFague make Christianity consistent with modern currents of ethics. Like Hitchens, they subject Christianity to ethical critique. Unlike Hitchens, they think revising Christianity salvages it so that it coheres with modern ethical demands. But this also assumes that we know what constitutes 'ethics', and then fit Christianity to it. This gives us an 'ethical Christianity', but not necessarily a 'Christian ethics'. The latter assumes that we do not begin by thinking of Christianity in terms of what we know of ethics, but that we think of ethics in terms of what we know of

Christianity. This does not mean that Christians and non-Christians cannot agree on what constitutes ethics, but it does mean that Christian ethics cannot shy away from the 'scandal of particularity' that is found in both Judaism and Christianity. That scandal is that God 'elects' a specific people in the world to effect God's mission: Israel, Jesus, and the Church. This is the doctrine of election.

The doctrine of election, whereby God freely chooses one particular people to effect God's will in the world, seems unethical, especially in light of Kant's categorical imperative that defines so much of modern ethics (and which will be discussed below). Yet neither Christianity nor Judaism can avoid doctrine, or the unique and definitive role particular people and places play in God's actions in the world. Rabbi David Novak understood this well when he wrote:

> Indeed, these claims, like 'God elects Israel' or 'God is incarnate in Jesus,' are what Judaism and Christianity are all about. In fact, Judaism requires Jews to die as martyrs rather than exchange Judaism for anything else, even something as similar to Judaism as Christianity. Christianity makes a similar claim on Christians. Martyrs are willing to die for what they believe to be the highest truth one could possibly know in this world, because without a commitment to the existence of truth, one cannot affirm the truth of God.

I think Rabbi Novak is correct about both Christianity and Judaism; you cannot have either religion without these doctrines. But this raises once again Hitchens's concern. Are religions such as Judaism and Christianity ethically, if not politically, dangerous? If you think you have truth, and you are willing to die for it, does that not contribute to divisions among the earth's inhabitants? Does it not produce an unethical 'tribalism and bigotry'? To answer this, we will need now to explore what we might mean by the term 'ethics'.

Chapter 1
The sources of Christian ethics

Having given some clarification as to what constitutes Christianity, we now consider 'ethics'. In so doing, we will also begin to develop the sources for Christian ethics. When Christianity arrives, 'ethics' is already well established, both in Judaism and in what became known as 'pagan' ethics. *Christian* ethics draws on both these traditions, preserving what is good and yet showing the limits to pagan ethics, and making claims for how Jesus 'fulfils', but does not destroy, Jewish ethics.

'Pagan' ethics

Ethics in the broadest sense is the rational pursuit of what is good and avoidance of that which is evil. It is a discipline and pursuit older than Christianity. Early Christians referred to it as 'pagan' wisdom, which was certainly not a term of endearment. Christians used the term critically, questioning whether 'pagan' wisdom had anything to teach them. After all, in his first letter to the Corinthians, St Paul asked the question, 'Has not God made foolish the wisdom of the world?' The implied answer was yes. This could cause an early theologian such as Tertullian (AD 160–225) to ask, 'What has Jerusalem to do with Athens?' In other words, what does the wisdom of the cross (Jerusalem) have to do with the philosophical and ethical tradition of Greeks like Plato or Aristotle? Tertullian's question should not cause us to think that

2. Raphael's *School of Athens*. Plato and Aristotle discuss the good in a context that resembles a Christian church. Raphael depicts Christianity's engagement with 'pagan' wisdom

the early church fathers dismissed the wisdom of 'pagan' ethics; they did not, not even Tertullian. They believed, as did the medieval theologians, that God had created a world that could be rationally understood, and that goodness was intrinsic to the reason present in creation. For this reason, wisdom should be sought wherever it was found, including ethical wisdom. Raphael's (1483–1520) famous painting of *The School of Athens* (reproduced in Illustration 2) that hangs in the Vatican Museum illustrates this well.

In this painting, Plato and Aristotle stand in the centre, surrounded by other famous philosophers. Plato points upwards and Aristotle extends his hand out on a level plane. The building in which they are walking resembles a church or a cross, demonstrating how faith and wisdom, even the wisdom of the 'pagans', can work together. We can only imagine why Plato points upward and Aristotle forward. It could be a sign of their different conceptions of the good. For Plato, the good is a 'form' that transcends the material reality of everyday. We need to see beyond such material reality in order to pursue the good. For Aristotle, the good is a form found in everyday things. We need to look to them in order to pursue the good. For both, the good is an object that produces desires in us. These desires cause us to seek the good, which is more than what produces the desires that start us on the journey, desires for pleasure, wealth, fame, and honour. None of these can satisfy the desire the good produces. If we stop at them, then we will fail to achieve our true end, the good.

Virtue

Pagan moral wisdom emphasized the place of 'virtue' for the successful pursuit of the good. As R. C. Hauser indicates, virtue is related to the 'excellence' (*arête*) a virtuous man (and it was primarily men who were thought to be virtuous in antiquity) exercises in the course of his life. It was originally linked to the virtue of courage, which was found primarily, albeit in a flawed manner, in Achilles. Ancient accounts of the virtues were related to stories about such men. Virtue is a power or potential in the human creature that is repeatedly exercised until it becomes part of who the person is. Just as an athlete trains so that she or he can 'naturally' run, swim, or cycle in a way alien to most people, so the virtues are 'excellences' that persons embody through involvement in certain activities. Such considerations gave rise to the 'cardinal virtues', which are justice, wisdom, courage, and temperance. The term 'cardinal' comes from the Latin, *cardo*, which can mean 'hinge' or 'axis'. The cardinal virtues provide a 'hinge' for the moral life, or give a person an 'axis' by which to live in the world. We can give definitions for each of these virtues, as Aristotle, Plato, and Cicero did. For instance, Cicero stated that everything 'morally right' (or *honestum* in Latin) 'arises from one of four sources', which are:

1) the full perception and intelligent development of the true (wisdom or prudence);
2) rendering to every man his due, and with the faithful discharge of obligations assumed (justice);
3) the greatness and strength of a noble and invincible spirit (courage);
4) the orderliness and moderation of everything that is said and done wherein consists temperance and self-control (temperance).

Although these definitions are helpful, they are best understood through the stories of their embodiment in characters. For instance, Aristotle uses the stories of Diomedes and Hektor to exemplify courage. Such stories are always local; you would need to live in a culture where people know the stories of Diomedes and Hektor to see how they exemplify the virtues. The exercise of virtue depends on local circumstances, just as riding a bicycle in a flat country produces different habits than riding in mountains. Likewise, what it meant to be a good Spartan would not necessarily be the same as a good Athenian. For Aristotle, the virtues require a particular form of civic life for them to make sense. This also meant certain persons were excluded from attaining the excellences – slaves, women, and some foreigners. Nonetheless, Aristotle did think that every person aimed for one thing in his or her actions, which was happiness. All moral action took place under its implicit or explicit pull. Happiness, or *eudaimonia* in Greek, was *the* good, without which human action would not make sense. This was the *telos*, the Greek word for 'end', which everyone and everything desired. For that reason, ancient virtue ethics is often called 'eudaimonistic' and 'teleological'. It assumes an end present in the nature of all things, for which they aim. The purpose of ethics, then, is to guide our lives to attain that end, an end that could be achieved by avoiding excesses and deficiencies of life. Virtue was a mean. For this reason, virtues could be designated as a mean between excess and deficiency. The following table shows some of the key virtues Aristotle discusses along with their deficiencies and excesses.

Deficiency	Virtue	Excess
Fear	Courage	Confidence or recklessness
Insensitivity to pleasures	Temperance or self-control	Self-indulgence
Stinginess	Generosity	Extravagance
Niggardliness	Magnificence	Vulgarity
Pettiness	High-mindedness	Vanity
Lack of ambition	The Nameless Virtue	Ambition
Apathy	Gentleness	Short temper
Grouchiness	Friendliness	Obsequiousness
Self-deprecation	Truthfulness	Boastfulness
Boorishness	Wittiness	Buffoonery
Any of the above	Justice, which implies proper regulations of all the above virtues. It sums up all the virtues.	Any of the above
Any of the above	Theoretical wisdom (concerned with things that are unchanging). It knows what is true.	Any of the above
Any of the above	Practical wisdom (concerned with things that can be other). It is 'deliberating well about what is good'.	Any of the above

Notice how Aristotle frames his discussion of the virtues through the four 'cardinal' ones. He first discusses courage and temperance, and concludes with justice and wisdom. The latter do not have specific deficiencies or excesses, but any deficiency or excess in the other virtues prohibits the proper exercise of justice or wisdom.

The virtues are not a 'compromise' between two vices, as if friendliness would require the right amount of grouchiness and obsequiousness. The vices are disordered desires, which are to be avoided. The virtues act as a guide to order our natural desires to their proper end of happiness. As Alasdair MacIntyre put it, the moral life begins with 'our nature as it is in itself', including its desires, and then transforms it to 'our nature as it should be'. This movement is what helps us make sense of laws and commands. They are not ends in themselves; they are intelligible because of the ends to which they direct and form our nature.

Natural law

The natural law was another ancient approach to ethics alongside virtue. Aristotle suggested such a law. He recognized that languages, customs, and laws differed among various societies. This could lead to laws that were merely set forth by a society, which would be 'positive law'. It has no greater justification than the will of that society. The 'law of nature' would be a law that was more foundational than these locally established laws; it was a law built into nature itself. The stoics were especially prone to consider the ethical life in terms of the 'natural law', and thought, unlike Aristotle, that the person truly in sync with the natural law would not be swayed from the good by external contingencies, like sickness, loss of property, or natural disasters.

Early and medieval Christianity, along with Judaism and Islam, developed the Greek and Roman traditions of the natural law, and this has an ongoing influence in modern Christian ethics. When Martin Luther King, Jr was imprisoned in Alabama for challenging the city's enacted legislation for segregation, he appealed to the doctrine of the natural law. In his famous letter from a Birmingham jail, quoting St Augustine, he wrote, 'an unjust law is no law at all'. This also has an ancient lineage in the Christian tradition. The Roman pagan Celsus charged Christianity with failing to honour the common wisdom that each nation has its own religion and ethics. Celsus wrote, 'the practices done by each nation are right when they are done in the way that pleases the overseers'. The Christian thinker Origen (AD 185–254) rejected this, along with Celsus's claim that the 'written laws of cities' were to be honoured more so than the 'ultimate law of nature' given by God. For Origen, if the former contradicts the latter, the former is to be ignored even if that requires 'dangers, troubles, death and shame'.

Christians and the virtues

How did Christian ethics relate to this ancient understanding of moral wisdom? Although natural law was not a central preoccupation among the church fathers, most of them found a place for virtue in the Christian life. St Athanasius (AD 296–373) reminded his readers that the monk St Anthony regularly admonished younger monks: 'do not be afraid to hear about virtue and do not be a stranger to the term'. St Ambrose (AD 340–97), like the 'pagan' stoic Cicero, wrote a treatise 'On the Duties'. It did not deny that Cicero and other ancient philosophers explained the virtues well, but Ambrose found patriarchs of the Old Testament, such as Abraham, Jacob, Joseph, Job, and David, the best exemplars of such virtues. He wrote:

> What duty connected with the chief virtues was wanting in these men? In the first place they showed prudence, which is exercised in the search of the truth, and which imparts a desire for full knowledge; next, justice, which assigns each man his own, does not claim another's, and disregards its own advantage, so as to guard the rights of all; thirdly, fortitude, which both in warfare and at home is

conspicuous in greatness of mind and distinguishes itself in the strength of the body; fourthly, temperance, which preserves the right method and order in all things that we think should either be done or said.

Notice how Ambrose used Cicero's understanding of the sources of the moral life and suggested that the patriarchs possessed them best. Like Athanasius, he affirmed the ancient virtues, but also re-contextualized them. Neither Achilles nor Socrates shows us the virtues; the biblical characters and saints do. Their stories now give the virtues their meaning.

It might be thought that the influential St Augustine (AD 354–430) rejected 'pagan' virtue; he is well known for designating 'pagan virtues' as 'splendid vices'. But it would be a mistake to think that he and other Christians did not draw on and develop this ancient tradition as well. He does not so much reject them as argue they are limited. This is not because he is worried about some otherworldly realm, but because he finds pagan ethics 'inadequate in themselves' for preserving and cultivating what is good in this life. Nevertheless, St Augustine also drew on the tradition of the pagan virtues and reordered them by making 'charity' their form. He wrote:

> As to virtue leading us to a happy life, I hold virtue to be nothing else than perfect love of God. For the fourfold division of virtue I regard as taken from four forms of love. For these four virtues (would that all felt their influence in their minds as they have their names in their mouths!), I should have no hesitation in defining them: that temperance is love giving itself entirely to that which is loved; fortitude is love readily bearing all things for the sake of the loved object, justice is love serving only the loved object, and therefore ruling rightly; prudence is love distinguishing with sagacity between what hinders it and what helps it. The object of this love is not anything, but only God, the chief good, the highest wisdom, the perfect harmony. So we may express the definition thus: that

temperance is love keeping itself entire and incorrupt for God; fortitude is love bearing everything readily for the sake of God; justice is love serving God only, and therefore ruling well all else, as subject to man; prudence is love making a right distinction between what helps it towards God and what might hinder it.

Augustine has radically revised the virtue tradition such that the love of God should order all our desires.

Much of the Christian tradition followed this practice of taking over the ancient tradition of pagan moral wisdom and re-narrating it in the context of the Christian faith. This would both affirm and transform the ancient virtues. They would not only be considered 'cardinal' or 'natural', but they would also be completed with 'theological' or 'infused' virtues, which were found in Scripture: faith, hope, and love. These virtues, because they draw us into the life of God, do not know an excess to be avoided; for God is infinite. God is 'excess'. The theological virtues then reorder all the virtues. This gave rise to the 'seven virtues' that are often depicted in Christian art.

Some eight centuries after Augustine, we find St Thomas Aquinas (1225–74) still drawing on the virtue tradition and giving it a more explicit foundation in Christian doctrine. The fresco by Andrea da Firenze (c. 1365) in the Spanish Chapel of the Church of Santa Maria Novella, Florence, known as *The Triumph of St Thomas Aquinas*, illustrates the seven virtues that are now to be read within the context of the Holy Scriptures open on Thomas's lap (Illustration 3).

He divided his most famous work, *Summa Theologia*, into three parts. The first part treats of God, the second of the movement of rational creatures to God, and the third of Christ, who as a man is the way to God. Aquinas treats moral wisdom in the second part, whereas much of his work on Christian doctrine is found in the first and third parts. They frame his re-narration of the virtue

3. *The Triumph of St Thomas Aquinas*: Thomas holds open the Scripture. Persons from the Old and New Testament surround him, and they and the Scriptures frame the virtues

tradition. Unfortunately, the second part of his *Summa* became divided from the first and third, circulating without them. This resulted in a failure to see how Aquinas had transformed the virtues by Christian doctrine. But even in the second part, he transforms the ancient understanding. For instance, after explaining the pagan virtues at length, which he called natural or acquired virtues, he then turned to the supernatural virtues and made a startling claim:

> It is therefore clear from what has been said that only the infused virtues are perfect, and deserve to be called virtues simply: since they direct man well to the ultimate end. But the other virtues, those, namely that are acquired, are virtues in a restricted sense, but not

simply: for they direct man well in respect of the last end in some
particular genus of action, but not in respect of the last end simply.

Here he argues that only the infused virtues are truly virtues; all
others are to be understood as 'virtues in a restricted sense'. They
can order our lives somewhat toward what is good, but they cannot
properly order them to our true end because the true end is now
friendship with the Triune God; something which Aristotle would
have found utterly objectionable. For him, true friendship could
only occur among equals. For Aquinas and the Christian tradition,
following the Gospel of John, we can now be friends with God
(John 15:15–16, New Revised Standard Version). Aquinas did not
deny the importance of the acquired virtues, but he insists that to
achieve our true end, we will need the infused virtues as well as
gifts, fruits of the Holy Spirit, and beatitudes. For him, Christian
ethics is much more gift than achievement, even though our will
must cooperate with the gift.

We will address more fully the theological virtues, gifts, fruits, and
beatitudes in the next section. The key to understanding the
oddness of this Christian ethic will be in making sense of
'hallowing', or making holy. To this point, we have traced all too
cursory a tradition of Greek moral wisdom and some central
Christian responses to it. But this is not the only tradition of ethics
to which Christian faith relates. It is more intimately related to
Judaism.

Jewish ethics: Torah as 'social project' and the Church as a 'social ethic'

Christian ethics finds its source in diverse means, but it primarily
emerges from the biblical narrative and especially the call of
Abraham and Sarah and subsequent creation of the Jewish people,
who received certain sacred possessions by which God would bless
all the nations, including the gift of the Divine Name, the Torah
(including the Ten Commandments), and the Tabernacle/Temple

as the place where heaven and earth meet. It is the dwelling-place of God on earth. These sources were essential for the emergence of Christian ethics, which assumes the social context of the Church. Without it, Christian ethics would be unintelligible. The Church continues the mission of Abraham and Sarah, which has as its goal nothing less than the 'Kingdom of God' coming on earth. The sources for Christian ethics, such as the Lord's Prayer, the Sermon on the Mount, the Theological Virtues, and the Sacraments, remind us of this goal, prepare the way for it, and witness to its coming.

The call of Abraham

Christian ethics arises from the calling of Abraham, which is found in Genesis 12. The first eleven chapters of that book are often called 'primal history'. They take ancient myths from other cultures and rewrite them from the perspective of Israel's call. For instance, the creation story draws upon, but significantly alters, the Babylonian myth of Marduk's conquest over Tiamet in the Enuma Elis. Whereas that myth has creation arising from Tiamet's dead body after Marduk kills her, the Genesis account of creation has no such violent contest in order for God to create. Elements from other myths can be found in the first eleven chapter of Genesis, but they have been subordinated to a larger creation narrative that assumes creation is fundamentally good. Creation is so good that God dwells in it, especially in the Garden of Eden, where God 'walks' and 'communicates' with Adam and Eve. But they disobey God and are expelled from the garden and therefore from God's presence. But God does not abandon his creation.

In the Old Testament, the Tabernacle and then the Temple represents the remnant of the garden as the dwelling-place of God. The Temple has three parts, the porch, or *ulam*; the holy place, or *hekal*; and the Holy of Holies, or *debir*, where God dwells. As Margaret Barker explains, the *hekal* of 'the Temple interior was a garden representing the heavenly garden on the mountain of God, the original Garden of Eden'. The *debir* is the place of God's presence, a presence lost after the Fall. In the Genesis account, a cherubim (angel) now guards the entrance to the garden. In the Temple, two cherubim flank the Ark of the Covenant in the Holy of Holies (*debir*), the place where God dwells. A curtain separates the *hekal* and *debir*. The high priest only passes from the *hekal* to the *debir* once each year. When he does so, he begins with a garment, which like the veil represents the earth, filled with the colours of flora and fauna. The seven lampstands in the *hekal* signify seven planets or the known creation. But passing through the veil, he takes on a garment that is pure white, for passing into the *debir* he passes into heaven, God's created dwelling-place. The priest's actions bring all of creation back to God, seeking to restore the original, primal harmony and order where God and creation dwell together, even if this now takes place in the Temple and not in the fullness of creation itself. That original order was so harmonious and peaceful that humans do not eat animals and animals do not eat each other. Only after the flood in the Noahic covenant of Genesis 9 does God permit humans to eat animals. Noah's ark was a sign of God's peaceable kingdom, a messianic vision of creatures living together in peace, another image of the Temple.

The American Quaker Edward Hick (1780–1849) presented such a vision in his painting *The Peaceable Kingdom* (Illustration 4). Lambs, lions, bears, and children live together without fear, as do Europeans and the native peoples of the Americas.

Noah's ark represents such a messianic vision. Animals do not need to be caged and separated from each other. It is not, as a *Far Side* cartoon humorously depicted it, where a gazelle is dead on the ark and Noah yells, 'who let the lions loose again?'.

The Noahic covenant

The covenant God makes with Noah is only one of many such covenants in the Scriptures, each of which has a different audience. Or at least, that is how these covenants become received in Jewish and Christian tradition. The Noahic covenant includes

4. Edward Hick's *Peaceable Kingdom*: it depicts God's intention for creation. The lion and lamb lie down together. A little child leads a lion. People are reconciled to each other and lie in peace

commandments that all the children of Noah, which is all of humanity, should observe. We find this in the Mishnah, which are the written works from oral tradition in rabbinic Judaism. In Tosefta '*Abodah Zarah* 8.4, it states, 'Seven commandments were given to the children of Noah: regarding the establishments of courts of justice, idolatry, blasphemy, fornication, bloodshed, theft [and the torn limb]'. What these seven commandments mean was disputed in the rabbinic tradition. They were interpreted as what should be expected from a righteous Gentile living in the Holy Land, as well as the basic morality one should expect from any human being. They are a basic Jewish ethic for Gentiles. They should establish courts of justice, avoid idolatry, blasphemy, sexual promiscuity, murder, stealing, and should observe certain food laws. (This is the reference to the 'torn limb'. How animals are prepared for consumption matters. Road kill shouldn't be eaten!) These

Noahic commandments were often reduced to three by Christians: avoid fornication, bloodshed, and blasphemy or idolatry.

When the early Christians had to decide how Gentiles were to be included in the Jewish covenant, they did so by reference to this Noahic ethic. We see this in the First Council at Jerusalem in Acts 15. Should the new Gentile believers keep the Torah as Jews? Should male converts be circumcised? After deliberation, James counsels that they are 'to abstain only from things polluted by idols and from fornication and from whatever has been strangled and from blood' (Acts 15:19). What was meant by 'from blood' is not clear. It most likely meant certain food laws like the 'torn limb' law. However, in the early Church these Noahic commandments became the basis for three sins for which repentance was not possible: fornication, idolatry or blasphemy, and murder; the 'torn limb' law became understood as a prohibition against shedding blood. Eventually, the Church allowed repentance even for these sins, although that would not occur until the 3rd century.

The City of God

Of course, the prehistory in Genesis 1–11 is not all peace, harmony, and goodness. The images of the peaceable kingdom are present in order to provide a sharp contrast with the world as it actually has become. We find evil, violence, and destruction. God does not cause evil in these stories. Nor does God need it in order to create. It occurs accidentally when human creatures bring it upon themselves. The 'Fall' of Adam and Eve conveys that all is not well, especially when it comes to human efforts to discern good from evil. Things continue to worsen among Adam and Eve's children. Cain kills his brother Abel, and God judges him, but not by making him a wanderer and exile as he fears. God protects him. In fact, his son Enoch builds the first city (Genesis 4:7).

The role of the 'city' in the Bible is very important. In one sense, as St Augustine recognized, the movement of Scripture is towards the 'City of God', from which Christian ethics emerges. Unlike most earthly cities, nations, and empires, God's calling of Israel is for the expressed purpose of building a 'city', 'nation', or 'house' where God dwells with people and people with God. We see this in the important juxtaposition of Genesis 11 and 12. Genesis 11 brings to a close the primeval 'history'. It does not end well. All human creatures have a common language and use their 'communion' with each other to build a city that will reach to the heavens, which is God's created dwelling-place. They seek to make a name for themselves, and in so doing, rival God. In turn, God judges them by dividing them up into nations and languages. Their city, 'Babel', remains unfinished.

> So the Lord scattered them abroad from there over the face of all the earth, and they left off building the city. Therefore it was called Babel, because there the Lord confused the language of all the earth; and from there the Lord scattered them abroad over the face of all the earth.

(Genesis 11:8–9)

Genesis 11 ends with an unfinished city. In one sense, the completion of this city, where God is the architect and not humanity, is what concerns Scripture most. It is why God calls Abraham. It marks a decisive turning in the biblical story. No longer do we find large mythical narratives; now we get a local, family history. In Genesis 12, God calls Abraham and makes the following promise to him:

> Go from your country and your kindred and your father's house to the land that I will show you. I will make of you a great nation, and I will bless you, and make your name great, so that you will be a blessing. I will bless those who bless you, and the one who curses you I will curse; and in you all the families of the earth shall be blessed.

(Genesis 12:1–2)

As this promise and blessing unfolds in the story of Israel, it takes on more and more concreteness. We discover Israel's call is

28

twofold: first, they are not to be like the other nations; second, they are not to be like the other nations for the sake of the nations. The election of Israel as God's chosen people establishes a mission for them, which has significance for all the peoples, cities, and families of the earth. They are called to live in such a way that Yahweh alone will be their leader. In order for them to live this way, they must first have an 'exodus'. They come out of slavery in the great city of Egypt and are given several things no other nation has. First, they are given the Divine Name, *ehyeh asher ehyeh* ('I am who I am'), which is the basis for the 'tetragrammaton', or four-letter name for God: YHWH. Second, they are given the Torah, which are the gracious commands by which Jews live, and in so doing make God's Name holy throughout the earth. Third, they are given the assurance of God's presence or 'glory' through specific worship regulations and practices.

The Divine Name and the Torah

God's Name is given to Moses in Exodus 3 while he is tending his father-in-law's flock. God speaks to him in a burning bush and sends him, as God sent Abraham, on a mission. God communicates with Moses by assuming the form of the bush without consuming it. We will discuss this odd form of communication below when we look at how the Holy Spirit is the 'principle of communion' that creates the Church, but now we focus more on what was communicated than the mode of communication. God tells Moses he must go back to Egypt, where the Jews are enslaved and from which Moses fled to escape punishment for killing an Egyptian, and tell Pharaoh to let God's people go. This is a very odd 'revolution'. God does not send him back armed, or tell him to begin a resistance movement. Moses simply uses the power of God's Word to tell Pharaoh the truth – 'these people you enslaved are God's people. They have a special mission. Let them go so they can fulfil it.' In order to let the Jewish people know God supports Moses, God gives him the Divine Name, a most sacred possession. The Jews finally leave Egypt and travel with God in the wilderness. There they receive a second sacred possession, the Torah. These are the commands by which they are to live. Although there are 613 such commands, the 'Ten Words', or Ten Commandments, crystallize the heart of the Torah. Living by these commands is how Jews fulfil the mission not to be like the other nations for the sake of the nations and in turn make God's Name holy throughout the earth. Christian ethics likewise makes no sense without the gift of the Torah.

The Ten Commandments are not unique. Other nations had commands by which they were to live, and some of those commands bear similarities to Yahweh's commands to the Jews. However, as Jean Louis Ska points out, all other commands were given under two conditions the Jews lacked. They were given under a determined monarchy within a fixed territory. These things were first in place and then laws were issued. Likewise, sanctions were noted for failure to keep the commands. God's call upon the Jews lacks these conditions as well as the threat of sanctions. The Torah is given in the desert without the presence of a king. The land and monarchy do not first constitute Jewish identity; the gift of the Torah does. This makes them unlike other nations. In fact, there is a rabbinic tale about the giving of the Torah to Israel that highlights this difference. God offers the Torah to the children of Esau but they reject it because it says 'Thou shalt not kill'. They say, 'This goes against our grain. Our father led us to rely only on the sword because he was told: *By the sword shalt thou live*' (Genesis 19:36). God then offers it to the children of Ammon and Moab, but they cannot abide by the command, 'Thou shalt not commit adultery' for that is their very origin. He offers it to the children of Ishmael, who refuse because of the command not to steal, which is how they make their living. Then 'at length He came to Israel. They have no such dramatic origin as these other nations and so they said: *We will do and hearken*' (Exodus 24:7). The fulfilment of Israel's mission requires a careful balance. Their calling will be unfulfilled if they maintain distinctiveness, but not as a blessing for the nations. Likewise, it will be unfulfilled if they lose distinctiveness by becoming just like the other nations. Observing the Commandments maintains the proper balance.

The Ten Commandments

Christians do not feel compelled to observe all 613 commandments. However, most are serious about keeping the Ten, even though the New Testament contains only a few references to them and nowhere cites them all. Christians and Jews share these in common, even when we number them differently. The table below lists the commands and how Jews, Reformed Christians, Eastern Orthodox, Catholics, Lutherans, and Anglicans divide them:

Prologue	
Jews	
Reformed Churches, Eastern Orthodox	I am the Lord your God, who brought you out of the land of Egypt, out of the house of slavery (Exodus 20:2).
Roman Catholics, Anglicans, Lutherans	
First Commandment	
Jews	I am the Lord your God, who brought you out of the land of Egypt, out of the house of slavery; You shall have no other Gods before me (Exodus 20:2).
Reformed Churches, Eastern Orthodox	You shall have no other Gods before me (Exodus 20:3).
Roman Catholics, Anglicans, Lutherans	I am the Lord your God, who brought you out of the land of Egypt, out of the house of slavery; You shall have no other Gods before me. You shall not make for yourself an idol, whether in the form of anything that is in heaven above, or that is on the earth beneath, or that is in the water

underneath the earth. You shall not bow down to them or worship them; for I the Lord your God am a jealous God, punishing children for the iniquity of parents, to the third and the fourth generation of those who reject me, but showing steadfast love to the thousandth generation of those who love me and keep my commandments (Exodus 20:2–6).

Second Commandment

Jews, Reformed Churches, Eastern Orthodox	You shall not make for yourself an idol, whether in the form of anything that is in heaven above, or that is on the earth beneath, or that is in the water underneath the earth. You shall not bow down to them or worship them; for I the Lord your God am a jealous God, punishing children for the iniquity of parents, to the third and the fourth generation of those who reject me, but showing steadfast love to the thousandth generation of those who love me and keep my commandments' (Exodus 20:3–6).
Roman Catholics, Anglicans, Lutherans	You shall not make wrongful use of the name of the Lord your God, for the Lord will not acquit anyone who misuses his name' (Exodus 20:7).

Third Commandment

Jews, Reformed Churches, Eastern Orthodox	You shall not make wrongful use of the name of the Lord your God, for the Lord will not acquit anyone who misuses his name' (Exodus 20:7).
Roman Catholics, Anglicans, Lutherans	Remember the Sabbath day, and keep it holy. Six days you shall labour and do all your work. But the seventh day is a Sabbath to the Lord your God; you shall not do any work – you, your son or your

daughter, your male or female slave, your livestock, or the alien resident in your towns. For in six days the Lord made heaven and earth, the sea and all that is in them, but rested the seventh day; therefore the Lord blessed the Sabbath day and consecrated it' (Exodus 20:8–11).

Fourth Commandment

Jews, Reformed Churches, Eastern Orthodox	Remember the Sabbath day, and keep it holy. Six days you shall labour and do all your work. But the seventh day is a Sabbath to the Lord your God; you shall not do any work – you, your son or your daughter, your male or female slave, your livestock, or the alien resident in your towns. For in six days the Lord made heaven and earth, the sea and all that is in them, but rested the seventh day; therefore the Lord blessed the Sabbath day and consecrated it (Exodus 20:8–11).
Roman Catholics, Anglicans, Lutherans	Honour your father and your mother, so that your days may be long in the land that the Lord your God is giving you (Exodus 20: 12).

Fifth Commandment

Jews, Reformed Churches, Eastern Orthodox	Honour your father and your mother, so that your days may be long in the land that the Lord your God is giving you (Exodus 20:12).
Roman Catholics, Anglicans, Lutherans	You shall not murder (Exodus 20:13).

Sixth Commandment

Jews, Reformed Churches, Eastern Orthodox	You shall not murder (Exodus 20:13).

| Roman Catholics, Anglicans, Lutherans | You shall not commit adultery (Exodus 20:14). |

Seventh Commandment

| Jews, Reformed Churches, Eastern Orthodox | You shall not commit adultery (Exodus 20: 14). |

| Roman Catholics, Anglicans, Lutherans | You shall not steal (Exodus 20:15). |

Eighth Commandment

| Jews, Reformed Churches, Eastern Orthodox | You shall not steal (Exodus 20:15). |

| Roman Catholics, Anglicans, Lutherans | You shall not bear false witness against your neighbour (Exodus 20:16). |

Ninth Commandment

| Jews, Reformed Churches, Eastern Orthodox | You shall not bear false witness against your neighbour (Exodus 20:16). |

| Roman Catholics, Anglicans, Lutherans | You shall not covet your neighbour's house (Exodus 20:17a). |

Tenth Commandment

| Jews, Reformed Churches, Eastern Orthodox | You shall not covet your neighbour's house; you shall not covet your neighbour's wife, or male or female slave, or ox, or donkey, or anything that belongs to your neighbour (Exodus 20:17). |

| Roman Catholics, Anglicans, Lutherans | You shall not covet your neighbour's wife, or male or female slave, or ox, or donkey, or anything that belongs to your neighbour (Exodus 20:17b). |

The first four Commandments (or three in the Catholic, Anglican, and Lutheran numbering) are called the 'first table' and they direct us to the proper love of God. The second table of the Commandments guides us to love our neighbour. Some of the differences in the numbering of the Ten are significant. For instance, Jews, the Reformed Christians, and the Eastern Orthodox separate the command to have no other gods from the one against idolatry. Roman Catholics, Anglicans, and Lutherans combine them into one, assuming that because no other gods actually exist other than the one true God, to have another god would therefore always be an act of idolatry. The older division found in Judaism may reflect a time when other 'gods' or spiritual powers were understood to be the source of various nations. The refusal to have such gods would then not be the same as idolatry; it would be to exchange YHWH for the gods of the nations. Idolatry would be to reduce YHWH to an image, like the nations do with their gods.

All Christians, like Jews, are supposed to be committed to these commands, but how they do so requires ongoing interpretation within the context of Jesus's 'fulfilment' of the Torah. The command not to make idols or images of God elicited great controversy in the 8th and then the 16th century, when some Christians opposed icons as a violation of the Commandment. The Second Council of Nicaea in 787 ruled that icons were not images or idols of God and could be venerated, which differed from being worshipped. The Reformers of the 16th century once again questioned the images in Roman Catholic churches. Some Reformers white-washed walls to remove the images. Sabbath-keeping is one that Christians would seem to violate at the command of Jesus; for he stated he was 'Lord of the Sabbath' (Matthew 12:8; Luke 6:5) and that the Sabbath was 'made for humankind' and not vice versa (Mark 2:27). This has caused many Christians to see a sharp distinction between the law found in the Old Testament and the gospel in the New. However, in both of these stories, Jesus appeals explicitly to the law against the Pharisees' tradition of putting a 'hedge' around the law and then making that hedge more important than the Torah itself. Jesus did not overthrow the Torah. In many ways, his interpretation of it was thoroughly Jewish.

Interpreting the Ten Commandments

Nevertheless, the role of the Ten Commandments in Judaism, Christianity, and Western culture is not identical. How are they to be understood? They make best sense when placed within the context of Israel's specific calling and mission, and we recognize that they constitute a 'social project'. The Ten Commandments constitute the social nature of God's people. For this reason, they were to be placed in the 'Ark of the Covenant', which was in the Holy of Holies (the *debir*) in the Tabernacle, the dwelling-place of God. When they are removed from that social location and made into something else, they can quickly lose their theological significance.

The comedian Stephen Colbert humorously exposed such loss in an interview with a US congressman, who co-sponsored a bill to have the Ten Commandments displayed in public buildings. This was a hotly contested issue in the US when the Supreme Court mandated removing them from courthouses, where they had been placed since 1943 by a campaign in the US and Canada for the purposes of a 'youth guidance project'. The assumption in 1943 was that troubled youth would benefit from observing the Ten Commandments displayed in public buildings. Some US citizens found the removal of the Ten Commandments objectionable and sought to reinstate them. Colbert interviewed one such congressman and asked him the reason for his bill. The congressman asked, 'Where better place could you have something like that than in a judicial building or in a courthouse?' To which Colbert responded, 'That is a good question. Can you think of any better building to put the Ten Commandments than in a public building?' The obvious answer was a church, temple, or synagogue, but the congressman did not consider any of these places. Instead, he responded, 'No, I think if we are totally without them, we will lose a sense of our direction.' Colbert then asked him to name the Ten Commandments. He could only name three.

This humorous exchange shows how the Ten Commandments can be reduced to something like a magic amulet that will supposedly fix lapses in morality without the necessary social context and practices that render them intelligible. Are the Ten Commandments intended as a 'natural' morality for all people irrespective of their faith, or do they primarily make sense in terms of the call of Abraham and the mission of Jesus? If it is the former, then Christian ethics will be a 'code' morality that asks people to obey commands without first becoming part of a people for whom those commands make sense. This could be like telling someone to live by a command, 'when you are on base and there are two outs and the batter has three balls and two strikes take off with the pitcher's release' without giving her the social context for such a command. That rule only makes sense if someone already understands or is involved in the game of baseball. If you don't know that social context, the rule makes no sense. So what is the social context that makes the Ten Commandments intelligible? Answering this requires telling the story of the Jews and how Christians came to make that story their own. In so doing, a key element will be the (very Jewish) prayer Christians pray everyday: 'Our Father, who art in heaven, hallowed be thy Name. Your kingdom come . . .' The purpose of the commands is to be part of the people who make God's Name holy by the way they live. In so doing, God comes to dwell with creatures, and creatures with God. This is why the Torah is a social project.

The formation of the Church as the context for Christian ethics: the Lord's Prayer

Like the Ten Commandments, the Lord's Prayer assumes the context of Christianity's shared Jewish past. As Brant Pitre notes, it has a 'single overarching theme: the hope for a New Exodus and the End of the Exile'. Both these themes arise from the Old Testament. 'New exodus' assumes God will repeat the act in the first exodus when God delivered Israel from slavery in Egypt and gave the Divine Name to Moses. God's message to Pharaoh says he is 'Father' to them; for God tells Moses to say to Pharaoh, 'Israel is my first-born son. I said to you, "let my son go that he may worship me. But you refused to let him go; now I will kill your firstborn son"' (Exodus 4:22–23). Here we find an analogy between Pharaoh as a father who will mourn the loss of his son and God who mourns the loss of Israel his son. To pray 'Our Father' assumes this relation. It is a prayer that locates us in Israel's history. As God once delivered Israel from Egypt, the hope for a 'new exodus' is that God will repeat this act.

The 'end of exile' assumes the return of the glory of God, and the restoration of Jews, to Jerusalem. The judgement that scattered Israel to various lands will be lifted and they will be restored; exile comes to an end. In the prophets, God claims that on this day, he will 'hallow' or 'make holy' his Name (Ezekiel 36:23; Isaiah 52:5–6, 7, 11–12; Zechariah 14:5, 9, 11; Micah 4:5–8). This is why Jesus teaches his disciples to pray, 'Our Father who art in heaven, hallowed be thy Name'.

The Lord's Prayer, like the Torah, is not just a prayer for private individuals. Both are 'social projects', or a 'social ethic'. They invite people into a way of living that will make God's name holy through the 'form' God's people take. The biblical scholar Gerhard Lohfink suggests that this is the crucial question the Bible addresses, 'What form shall the people of God take?' The form the people take varies. First is the 'people of God as tribal society without a king'. This fulfils the call not to be like the other nations, but it is not always as a blessing for the other nations. Israel is given sacred possessions by which it is to live, not only the Divine Name and the Torah, but also regulations as to how they are to approach and use these possessions. They are to construct an 'Ark of the Covenant', which is overlaid with gold and has four rings on its feet, two on each side, where poles can go in order for it to be carried (Illustration 5). The glory of God will reside in this Ark and the

5. The Ark of the Covenant: the dwelling-place of God. The Torah is placed in the Ark

covenant made with Israel is placed in it (Exodus 25:10–16). A mercy seat of pure gold is placed on top of the Ark, with two gold cherubim surrounding it. God meets with the Jews at this place:

> There I will meet with you, and from above the mercy seat,
> from between the two cherubim that are on the ark of the
> covenant, I will deliver to you all my commandments for the
> Israelites.
>
> (Exodus 25:22)

Before the Ark stands a table for the bread of presence and the lampstand with seven lamps, which, as mentioned above, symbolize creation. The bread of presence is set on the table before the Lord. All of this is placed in a 'tabernacle' made up of ten curtains, which includes the three courts. One curtain made with blue, purple, and crimson yarn separates the Ark of the Covenant and the mercy seat, which are in the Holy of Holies, from the table and lampstand that are in 'the holy place' (Exodus 26:31–37). The colours signify creation. After everything is constructed, Scripture provides an account of a beautiful 'theophany' (manifestation of God) similar to the transfiguration of Jesus in the New Testament (Mark 9:2–8):

> Then the cloud covered the tent of meeting, and the glory of the Lord filled the tabernacle. Moses was not able to enter the tent of meeting because the cloud settled upon it, and the glory of the Lord filled the tabernacle. Whenever the cloud was taken up from the tabernacle, the Israelites would set out on each stage of their journey; but if the cloud was not taken up, then they did not set out until the day that it was taken up.

> (Exodus 40:34–6)

Here we see God sojourning with Israel as their guide and leader, dwelling in a tabernacle.

But this is not the only, or final, form Israel takes in Scripture, for it is unstable. It is for a people of promise on their way to a land. The next form, 'the people of God as a nation', gains stability. Israel inherits the land and receives a king. Some Christian ethicists see it as the basis for a proper political theology because it gives the Law the stability it needs. The monarchy is the origin of a proper political authority that provides a context within which proper judgements can be executed. Nevertheless, Scripture portrays the monarchy as a mixed 'gift'. The elders of Israel ask the prophet Samuel for it when he is old and they don't trust his sons. Samuel prays and God answers him:

> Listen to the voice of the people in all that they say to you; for they have not rejected you, but they have rejected me from being king over them. Just as they have done to me from the day I brought them

40

up out of Egypt to this day, forsaking me and serving other gods, so also they are doing to you.

(I Samuel 8:7–9)

Here the king is 'given' as a judgement against the people. God gives them what they want, but it is a rejection of their call. Samuel warns the people what this will mean. The king will take their sons 'to make his implements of war' and their daughters 'to be perfumers and cooks and bakers'. He will take the best of their fields, vineyards, and other forms of property. Nonetheless, the people demand a king. The reason why is intriguing – 'so that we also may be like the other nations, and that our king may govern us and go out before us and fight our battles' (I Samuel 8:20). They want to become like the other nations.

Monarchy and temple

Along with monarchy and kingship comes the temple. The telling of this story is poignant. It begins like this:

Now when the king was settled in his house, and the Lord had given him rest from all his enemies around him, the king said to the prophet Nathan, 'See now I am living in a house of cedar but the ark of God stays in a tent.' Nathan said to the king, 'Go, do all that you have in mind; for the Lord is with you.

(2 Samuel 7:1–3)

Here for the first time we find Israel 'settled' and at 'rest'. Is this good? Any answer to that question will have to be subtle, for the story is ambiguous. On the one hand, this was God's promise to David. But on the other, God still dwells in a tent ready for transport, the opposite of being settled. David decides that since he is settled and lives in a fine house, God should as well. The prophet Nathan, without consulting God, tells David God is with him. God speaks to him that night with contrary plans.

> Go and tell my servant David: Thus says the Lord: Are you the one to build me a house to live in? I have not lived in a house since the day I brought up the people of Israel from Egypt to this day, but I have been moving about in a tent and a tabernacle. Wherever I have moved about among the people of Israel, did I ever speak a word with any of the tribal elders of Israel, whom I commanded to shepherd my people Israel saying, 'Why have you not built me a house of cedar?'

(2 Samuel 7:5–7)

Much like the ambiguity found in the establishment of the monarchy, here we also find ambiguity in the people formed as a temple community. In fact, God reverses David's desire. Instead of David building him a house, God will build David a house.

> Moreover the Lord declares to you that the Lord will make you a house. When your days are fulfilled and you lie down with your ancestors, I will raise up your offspring after you, who shall come forth from your body, and I will establish his kingdom. He shall build a house for my name, and I will establish the throne of his kingdom forever. I will be a father to him, and he shall be a son to me.

(2 Samuel 7:11–14)

Here we find once again the central task of a Christian (and Jewish) ethic – to build, or rather be built into, a 'house' where God and creatures dwell together, a city where God's name is sanctified and God's kingdom established. The intimacy between God and his people will be that of 'father' and 'son'. This is why Christians pray, 'Our Father who art in heaven, thy kingdom come, thy will be done, on earth as it is in heaven'.

Exile

Of course, all does not end here, nor does it end well. On the one hand, the monarchy, land, and temple are gifts from God to Israel.

On the other hand, they are ambiguous. Do they fulfil the call to Abraham? Has Israel come out from the nations in order to be a blessing to the nations, or has it simply become like the other nations? Eventually, everything is taken away – land, monarchy, and temple. Israel is led into exile, into the 'diaspora'. Most peoples lose their identity and assimilate once they are exiles. Israel's stories, stories such as those found in the Book of Daniel, are about resisting such assimilation. The call not to be like other nations now takes on a new urgency and meaning. We see this in the Psalms, even those which express genuine anger, such as this one that laments the exile to Babylon:

> By the rivers of Babylon –
> there we sat down and there we wept
> when we remembered Zion.
> On the willows there we hung up our harps.
> For there our captors asked us for songs, and our tormentors
> asked for mirth, saying, 'Sing us one of the Songs of Zion!'
> How could we sing the Lord's song in a foreign land?
> If I forget you, O Jerusalem, let my right hand wither!
> Let my tongue cling to the roof of my mouth,
> if I do not remember you,
> if I do not set Jerusalem above my highest joy
>
> (Psalm 137:1–6)

The psalmist continues by proclaiming 'beatitude' for any who take their captors' babies 'and dash them against the rock'. Of course, such a violent cry is not intended as a moral prescription. It expresses an ultimate sense of loss. It is a haunting, plaintive, albeit deeply disturbing cry.

If the Torah is a social project, then how can it exist when Israel loses all the identifying markers of its sociality – land, monarchy, temple? But this is similar to the state in which the Jews received the Torah in the first place. Here takes place an amazing event.

In the diaspora, Israel gains a new-found sense of its calling. By gathering to remember Torah and hope for new exodus and the end of exile – 'next year in Jerusalem' – Israel rediscovers its calling. Jesus's mission takes place in the context of this hope.

Jesus's mission

The Christian Gospel is not that complicated. Jesus announces the Kingdom of God, gathers twelve men, heals, casts out demons, teaches, eats at other people's homes, and journeys towards Jerusalem. There he gets himself into serious political trouble and dies at the hands of the Roman state through crucifixion. The charge levelled against him was 'King of the Jews'. Jesus was not killed because he told people to be kind and loving. Surely neither the Roman leaders nor some Jewish elders were so utterly devoid of humanity that they conspired to kill Jesus because he taught such an innocuous, banal, and sentimental message. Something more profound than that got him killed. Gathering twelve disciples, heading for Jerusalem, claiming the power to forgive sins, and challenging the temple were all provocative acts he did that ended in his crucifixion. Gathering twelve disciples was a sign of the restoration of Israel. Heading for Jerusalem became a witness about the return of God's glory through a new exodus. Claiming to forgive sins was something only God could do and brought about the charge of blasphemy. Finally, challenging the temple was to question the form God's people should take. Jesus claims that his body itself will be the 'new temple'.

Through his crucifixion and resurrection, most Christians consider Christ's body to be the dwelling-place where heaven and earth, God and creatures, meet. His body is then mediated to others through the Word (Scripture) and Sacrament so that they become Christ's body. This is why most Christians speak of a threefold form to Christ's body. The first is the Risen, historical body that bears the wounds of sin eternally and sits at the right hand of God (acknowledging, of course, that this is metaphorical since God has no hands). The second is the Eucharist, or Lord's Supper, which is distributed to the faithful and also referred to as the 'body of Christ'. The third is the people this Sacrament, along with the Word, makes possible – the Church, which is also called 'the body of Christ'. This body is now to be distributed throughout the world as a catholic (universal) reality. Like Israel's mission, the Church's universal mission is to be distinct for the sake of all the nations. It does this by embodying and bearing witness to the 'blessed' or happy life Jesus proclaims.

The beatitudes, theological virtues, gifts, and fruits

As previously mentioned, ancient virtue ethics assumed the true end of life was happiness. Most Christians found what Robert Wilken called 'a serendipitous congruence of the Bible and the wisdom of the Greeks and Romans' with respect to a life of beatitude. Christians thought they found the true happiness the Greeks yearned for in Jesus and the way of life he called 'blessed'. The 'eudaimonistic' ethics of the ancient Greeks was fulfilled in the beatitudes Jesus announced in his Sermon on the Mount. It might not be too improper to suggest that until the Reformation this 'serendipitous congruence' was the basis for Christian ethics. Take, for instance, Thomas Aquinas's understanding of the moral life. It brings together two mountains, Mount Sinai, where God gives the Torah to Moses, and the unnamed Mount where Jesus pronounces certain ways of being and/or acting as 'blessed'. The two mountains are set over each other like a palimpsest where the beatitudes from the Sermon on the Mount complete or fulfil the Torah. They come together in that the beatitudes are acts that perfect the law.

Bringing together the Sixth Commandment, 'thou shalt not commit murder', and the seventh beatitude, peaceableness, shows how this works. Let us assume I get up in the morning and query whether I should kill my neighbour, who is particularly annoying. I do a cost–benefit analysis, weighing the pros and cons of violating the Sixth Commandment. After rational deliberation, I decide it is better not to kill my neighbour, perhaps because I fear the consequences, or because as a religious professional it would be bad for my career. Have I kept the law? The answer is yes and no. Yes, it is true I did not violate the Commandment. This is a good thing and should not be treated contemptuously. It could be the beginning of the acquired virtue of justice. But the answer is also no. The law has not truly been kept, for the purpose of the law is not merely to observe Commandments but to hallow God's Name. The beatitude of peaceableness perfects my actions when it would not even occur to me to violate the Sixth Commandment. I wouldn't even need to know the Commandment because it is now written in my very being. Few of us arrive at this stage in our life, and this is why Aquinas calls us 'wayfarers'. We are people on the 'way' to being 'citizens' of God's blessed city, where this way of life rules.

The terms 'wayfarer' and 'citizen' are important. They remind us that virtues, gifts, beatitudes, and fruits are much more than an individual, internalized spirituality. For just as the natural virtues are necessary for the proper functioning of life in a family or city, so the theological virtues, gifts, beatitudes, and fruits are necessary for life in the 'City of God', the New Jerusalem. This is an important biblical theme. It is found throughout the Sermon on the Mount in Matthew 5–7 where Jesus says, 'blessed are *they* for *theirs* is the Kingdom of heaven', and 'you [plural] are the light of the world, a city built on a hill' (Matthew 5:14), as well as 'those' who build a lasting house (Matthew 7:26–7). These images of a kingdom, city, house, or holy nation are nearly interchangeable throughout Scripture. They are the basic context for any Christian ethics, for they are the first fruits of the fulfilment of God's mission to the world, the Kingdom come. The Book of Revelation speaks of its consummation at the end of time:

> Then I saw a new heaven and a new earth; for the first heaven and the first earth has passed away, and the sea was no more. And I saw the

holy city, the new Jerusalem, coming down out of heaven from God, prepared as a bride adorned for her husband. And I heard a loud voice from the throne saying, 'See the home of God is among mortals. He will dwell with them as their God; they will be his peoples, and God himself will be with them'.... I saw no temple in the city, for its temple is the Lord God the Almighty and the Lamb. And the city has no need of sun or moon to shine on it, for the glory of God is its light and its lamp is the Lamb. The nations will walk by its light and the kings of the earth will bring their glory into it. Its gates will never be shut by day – and there will be no night there.

(Revelation 21:1–3, 22–26)

Here is a vision of the fulfilment of the call to Abraham. As a blessing to all the nations, this city is not to be like them even as it welcomes all that is good in them into its gates.

The theological virtues of faith, hope, and love sustain us 'on the way' to that city. Love remains when it arrives. The beatitudes are the city's perfections. The gifts and fruits of the Spirit make possible its achievement. The beatitudes are as follows:

1. *Poverty of spirit*	It is a poverty that frees us from external goods, whether riches or honours.
2. *Meekness*	It resists the lure of sensual appetites such as violence.
3. *Mournfulness*	It is a willingness to lose and therefore mourn things that others desire.
4. *Righteousness*	This is the justice that should rule in our relations with others.
5. *Mercifulness*	It is the preference we should show to those who are miserable and poor for no other reason than that they are poor.

6. *Purity of heart*	This is a simplicity that seeks God for God's own sake.
7. *Peaceableness*	It is the blessing that should come from a proper ordering of both one's relations to others and within one's self.
8. *Persecution for righteousness' sake*	This is an odd beatitude. If someone embodies all seven other beatitudes, this most likely results as long as we are still wayfarers. The person's life will become 'Christoform', which means she or he may be persecuted as Christ was.

These beatitudes were laid out with corresponding virtues and gifts in the Christian tradition, but never with a consistency such that they offered precise advice on what to do in any or every situation. They set forth a vision of what God's holiness looks like when embodied by God's creatures. In fact, as John Wesley and many others recognized, beatitudes, gifts, and fruits first and foremost characterize Christ's righteousness. He gives them to us because he alone perfectly embodied them, he is their source and can communicate them to others.

The place of the beatitudes in traditional Christian ethics cannot be overstated. The beatitudes are considered the 'acts', or 'works', of the virtues and gifts. They are the preparation for life as God intends, which we have inchoately in this life but will be perfected in the life to come. Thomas gives us the reason for these beatitudes, 'Because when a man begins to make progress in the acts of the virtues and gifts, it is to be hoped that he will arrive at perfection, both as a wayfarer, and as a citizen of the heavenly kingdom.'

How the seven gifts were distinguished from the theological virtues was debated in Christian ethics. Both were named from Scripture. The theological virtues come from I Corinthians 13; the gifts from Isaiah 11:2, 3. The gifts came to be viewed as 'higher perfections'

6. Jastrow's famous duck-rabbit. It shows how one thing can be two different things based on the perception that someone has

that made someone 'amenable to divine inspiration'. The theological virtues, even though they were infused from the Holy Spirit, were then intrinsic principles that moved the human creature by working on his natural principles of motion. Like the virtues, the gifts worked by ordering reason and the will (or desire), but they do this more so from without, by drawing us into God's own life. Four of the gifts perfect reason: they are wisdom, knowledge, understanding, and counsel. Three perfect the appetite: they are fortitude, piety, and fear. These gifts can also be natural or acquired virtues for each is located in human nature. As gifts, however, they are more than natural. Thus the relation between the natural virtues and the gifts is similar to Jastrow's duck-rabbit (Illustration 6).

Viewed under one aspect, the image looks like a duck; viewed under another, it is a rabbit. Yet both are contained in the same image. Analogically, wisdom and the other gifts have a similar form. They can be seen as merely natural and acquired, and as such should be affirmed. But Christian theologians claim that the relation between God and creatures is such that humans and God can both be the cause of a 'virtue' without divine and human agency being in competition. Thus these gifts are also divine *gifts*. As Aquinas puts it: 'Wisdom is called an intellectual virtue, so far as it proceeds from the judgement of reason: but it is called a gift, according as its work proceeds from the Divine prompting.'

The beatitudes and fruits of the Spirit are likewise distinguished from the theological virtues and gifts largely because they name different means of movement towards the end of happiness. The fruits of the Spirit are listed in Galatians 5: love, joy, peace, patience, kindness, goodness, faithfulness, gentleness, and self-control. They are similar to the beatitudes, and all beatitudes are fruits, but not all fruits are beatitudes. The difference is that fruits are 'virtuous deeds' which bring 'delight', but beatitudes are 'perfect works'. They are the fulfilment, perfection, or completion of the law.

Chapter 2
The history of Christian ethics

Christian ethics emerges out of the shared Jewish and Christian mission to make God's name holy throughout creation by 'building' a 'city' or 'house'. This requires a twofold approach to ethics, which can best be characterized by the call to Abraham: 'do not be like the other nations . . . for the sake of the nations.' This section traces the historical development of Christian ethics as it addresses both concerns.

The first section, 'do not be like the other nations', develops the patterns or forms of living those who voluntarily enter into this mission are called to embody. Ethics here is 'habituation' and 'infusion'. Habituation assumes that there are things we can do in order to 'put on' the life of Christ. Yet habituation alone is insufficient; Christian ethics also requires 'infusion'. It affirms that no matter how much we do or act rightly, the Christian life is never an achievement of our own apart from grace, which is a communication of the Holy Spirit. This requires attention to worship, and especially the development of 'penance', which is the historical source that gave rise to Christian ethics. Penance holds together both habituation and infusion; it requires that we do some things and turn away from others in order to receive what is already given to us in baptism.

The second section, '. . . for the sake of the nations', negotiates the diverse relations between those who voluntarily enter into the mission and those who do not. It asks the question of the relation between the Church and the 'nations'. This too is crucial to Christian ethics; it is a source of some of its greatest contributions as well as its significant failures.

The first section: 'do not be like the other nations. . .'

The basic pattern to Sunday worship discloses the shape of Christian ethics. This basic pattern has an ancient lineage. Robert Wilken argues that with 'little alteration' the liturgy found in the work of Justin Martyr (AD 100–65) has been present throughout Christian churches until the Reformation. That liturgy had five key elements:

1st: 'Biblical readings interspersed with prayers and psalms';
2nd: 'Exposition of the text' as a 'sermon' or 'homily';
3rd: Common prayers;
4th: Greeting with a kiss of peace;
5th: Bread, wine, and water are then brought forward and thanksgiving offered.

These five elements exist within a fourfold movement acknowledged by the World Council of Churches as the basic form of Christian worship. The first movement is the gathering. People leave their homes and enter into the church, gathered as a new community. Baptism initiates people into this new community. Every baptism is a mini-exodus where sin and slavery are left behind and the believer takes on the life of Christ, participating in his death and resurrection symbolized by the water of baptism. The gathered community receives the name of God in order to be reminded why they gather; this is why the first act of gathering normally invokes the Triune Name: 'In the Name of the Father, the Son and the Holy Spirit, Amen.'

The second movement is the reading and proclaiming of Holy Scripture. The readings give shape to the community as it is reminded that all these words are necessary for its ongoing mission and identity. They are followed with proclamation to encourage and exhort those gathered. The Word read and proclaimed demands response, so the third movement is various responses to the Word, which come in the form of confession, prayers, altar calls, and the Holy Eucharist, or Lord's Supper. The fourth and final act of worship is the sending forth. Those who have been gathered are now sent into the world to live as people marked by the Spirit. They are called from 'the nations' only to be equipped to be sent back to them.

The purpose of the liturgy: the Church's four marks

The purpose of the liturgy is to make people holy so that they in turn make God's Name holy; this is why every gathering for worship invokes the prayer – 'hallowed be thy Name'. To make God's Name holy is the work of the Holy Spirit, who helps the Church become what it is called to be, which is characterized by four marks: unity, holiness, catholicity, and apostolicity. Unity should characterize the Church's common life. Holiness is a feature of its nearness to God's goodness. Catholicity states that it is 'universal'; no particular time or place alone defines it. As G. K. Chesterton said, 'Christianity is a democracy of the dead'. Apostolicity is a 'task' by which the Church always seeks to keep faith, with its origin in the 'apostolic witness', primarily attested in Scripture. The Holy Spirit breathes life into the Church in order for it to embody these four marks.

The Spirit, writes Yves Congar, 'is the extreme communication of God himself, God as grace, God *in us* and, in this sense, God outside himself'. This word 'communication' is significant. The Spirit *communicates* God's presence by uniting communicator and communicated. It is therefore the 'principle of communion'. I briefly mentioned this in discussing the giving of the Divine Name in Exodus 3. Just as the Spirit communicated with Moses by taking the form of, but not consuming, the burning bush, so the Spirit communicates with that which is not God – creation – by bringing it into unity with God without losing the distinction between God and creatures. The symbol for the Spirit is often a flame.

The four marks of the Church are not mere sociological claims for the Church's ethical superiority, but theological descriptions of grace received and tasks set for the Church. Even the physical structure of churches participates in these four marks. Congar writes:

> The Church, which is the house of the living God, is the sacrament of salvation for mankind. It is not simply liturgy offered to God, but also a sign of God's love for men and of his kingdom. Even the structures that are also known as 'churches' have this part to play in our towns and villages.

Architecture matters. Think of the community in which you live; what gives it its 'orientation'? The philosopher Albert Borgmann reminds us that the term 'orientation' arose from the way cathedrals once shaped daily life in the West. They were built pointing towards the east, bearing witness to where Christian hope was directed – towards the homeland of Christ who would one day return. When Christians would stand to worship, they would have a similar orientation. The centrality of these buildings also gave shape to everyday life in villages and cities. Although the shopping centre with its easy access, or the fast-food restaurant with its quick availability, may 'orient' daily life in many of our cities and villages today, the presence of churches often still points to a different orientation that continues to make up the architecture of everyday life, gathering people daily and weekly for celebration of God's presence.

Of course, for most Christian churches, this witness does not take place without the human creature's willing participation. The building alone is insufficient; people must consent to the Spirit's work, which is why they stand and make confession, pray and go forward to receive the Eucharist. Nevertheless, any observant person would readily recognize that those so formed do not always embody the marks of the Church in their common life. This puzzled many in the early Church. If the Spirit is the actor in these events and people consent to the Spirit's work, why do they continue to do evil? The possibility that a person could repent for sins after baptism was controversial.

Penance or repentance

The Church was depicted as a 'ship' sailing through virulent waters of chaotic evil. Baptism gave you entrance into the ship; to sin was to jump out of that ship back into the waters, which for some would forfeit the redemption baptism brought about. In some places in the early Christianity apostasy, fornication or adultery and murder excluded one from the possibility of repentance after baptism. Eventually, repentance for even these sins could be achieved, although they were still taken to be gravely serious. So the understanding of the Christian moral life developed. Early on it assumed that after baptism Christians would not commit such grave sins and therefore could not be readmitted into the community. Later even such grave sins could be forgiven before and after baptism. The specific discipline of Christian ethics arises from pastors and theologians trying to figure out how to make sense of the sins that arise after baptism and whether they should or should not exclude someone from the Eucharist.

Baptism is an unrepeatable event whereby a person becomes a member of Christ's body, the Church. This gives him or her access to the Eucharist, which is a repeatable feast. As baptism symbolizes the once and for all exodus from slavery, so the Eucharist, or Lord's Supper, symbolizes the manna from heaven, which nourishes the 'wayfarers' moving towards God's 'New Jerusalem'. After baptism and before Eucharist is the necessary practice of 'repentance', or 'penance'. It is to be regularly repeated. Penance requires discerning what constitutes the good, or the holy, that baptism brings, which is why we first discussed the sources of Christian ethics in the gifts, beatitudes, the natural or acquired and the infused virtues. Once these are acknowledged, which, as we mentioned above, are found primarily in the righteousness of Christ, then those sins or vices that detract from them can also be acknowledged. St Augustine demonstrated this in his *Confessions* when he wrote, 'for love of your love I will retrace my wicked ways'. In other words, sin and vice are the lack of something that is much greater than them. Vice does not stand on its own; it is parasitic on virtue, its lack.

Deadly vices

We easily become fascinated with the vices and forget that the mere avoidance of them is not the purpose of Christian ethics. Perhaps this is why we have so many powerful movies and literary forms about the seven deadly vices (the film *Seven* comes to mind), but fewer art forms that show the same fascination with the beatitudes or the theological virtues (although the film *Joyeux Noel* would certainly be such a form). Vice seems to fascinate us more than virtue. The seven deadly vices were regularly present in manuals which priests used to help people identify sin. They are pride, covetousness, lust, gluttony, sloth, anger, and envy. Pride is 'the inordinate appetite for one's excellence'. Pride despises the good that comes to one's neighbours, friends, and enemies because the prideful person fears that the good given to them will detract from his or her own excellence. Covetousness is 'the inordinate love of temporal things'. Like the prideful person, the covetous person fears loss, not loss of status but loss of temporal goods. He is so led by this fear that he lives a life of deceit, doing all in his power to insure his own security against that of his neighbours. Lust is 'the inordinate appetite for sexual pleasure'. It should not be equated with sexual desire itself. Lust is a vice that leads one to dominate, consume, and destroy the other for one's own gratification. Gluttony (and drunkenness) is 'the inordinate indulgence in food or drink'. It is the desire to consume all the time and never know satisfaction. Sloth is the lack of sufficient desire to fulfil one's obligations. If lust and gluttony are an overabundance of disordered desires, sloth is the lack of appropriate desire. Anger is 'the inordinate inclination to take revenge'. Envy is the 'willful sadness on account of the good of another, whether temporal or spiritual, regarded as diminishing one's own good'.

These vices, like the virtues, might appear to be merely an ethic for individuals, but that would be to misunderstand them. The Anglican priest John Wesley (1703–91), who started the Methodist movement, recognized this in his commentary on the beatitudes. He wrote: 'I shall endeavor to show that Christianity is essentially a social religion, and that to turn it into a solitary religion is indeed to destroy it.' He gives an example of what he means in the beatitude of 'meekness', of which he writes, 'as it implies mildness, gentleness and long-suffering, it cannot possibly have a being . . . without an intercourse with other men. . . . So that to attempt turning this into a solitary virtue is to destroy it from the face of the earth.' The beatitudes require living in proximity with others. They cannot but involve questions of sex, war, economics, family, and so on – all of which are crucial social matters. Meekness, like the hunger for justice, requires a social context for its intelligibility. That context is found both in the Church and in the intersection between the Church and the world.

From penitentials to canon law, manuals, and the Protestant revolt

Historically, penance gave rise to Christian ethics. Irish monks confessed to each other in private, and then carried this practice with them on their missionary journeys throughout Europe. To assist this process, books known as *penitentials* were written which listed known sins and what should be done to remedy them. These books are an early, albeit strange, expression of Christian ethics. They mix local customs with theological and biblical convictions. Take, for example, the 7th-century Anglo-Saxon *Penitential of Theodore*. Some of its rules are odd, some seem overly rigorous, and others quite lenient. The odd rules are found in the dietary penances. Anyone who 'eats unclean flesh or a carcass that has been torn by beasts shall do penance for forty days'. Here we still find the 'torn limb' law of the Noahic covenant. Dietary penitentials can also be found with respect to eating or drinking where a dog, cat, mouse, or bird accidentally contaminated the food or liquid. Discovering a dog 'contaminated' one's food would seem to be penance enough without tacking on something more! In this penitential, masturbation required penance for three years, while murder only seven to ten. Penance would usually involve certain kinds of fasting as well as abstaining from the Eucharist.

Because of their arbitrary nature and lack of systematization, the penitentials created problems within the Church. Eventually, they were subject to the Carolingian reforms (8th and 9th centuries, initiated by Charlemagne), and then later an effort was made to regularize penitential practice in Gratian's decretum, which was the first attempt to systematize the arbitrary and conflicting canons concerning the moral life. It led to the development of canon law, which assisted the process of discerning good from evil and became one of the bases for 'rights' in Western society.

The Fourth Lateran Council, 1215, marked the end of medieval penance and the beginning of modern penance. It made possible a 'tariff system' of penance whereby penance became an end in itself. Individual auricular confession and the priest's absolution represented a growing cost–benefit analysis of sin and reward, whereby the Christian moral life is reduced to an accountant's ledger with sins on one side and penances as payment for those sins on the other. Manuals of confession were produced which focused on those acts alone that violated certain laws and how confessors were to lead their confessees into a thorough examination of conscience. Many Catholics and most Protestants found this system wanting. Catholics reformed the manualist tradition at Vatican II, which for them is the twenty-first ecumenical council held from 1962 to 1965.

Luther and the Lutherans' protest

Martin Luther, rightly or wrongly, thought that much of Christian ethics of the later Middle Ages resulted in a 'gallows sorrow' that was based on fear rather than the love of God. He protested against a corrupt form of penance that resulted in a minimalist and juridical conception of the moral life. When he was reconsidering the sacraments, Luther seemed ambiguous on whether penance should be a sacrament. In 1519, he wrote: 'The sacrament of penance renews and points out again the sacrament of baptism.' However, Luther rejected the long-standing tradition via Tertullian, Jerome, Augustine, and Aquinas that spoke of penance as a 'second plank', which he thought diminished the efficacy of baptism. He feared the practice of penance would prevent fully trusting in 'the first plank, or the ship', which was baptism. He feared any account of 'habituation' would lead Christians to trust in themselves rather than in grace alone. To think that acts of penance restored baptismal grace could too easily make grace dependent upon human works.

Luther could so emphasize the promise present in baptism that law became something overwhelmingly negative. This led to a 'forensic justification' whereby persons are forgiven by having God's righteousness imputed to, but not inherent in, them. So Luther stated that God 'pledges himself not to impute to you the sins which remain in your nature after baptism, neither to take them into account nor to condemn you because of them'. Instead, God 'winks at our sins' and regards us 'as if' we were sinless. Sin is so 'overruled by our baptism that it does not condemn us and is not harmful to us'. This will give a different conception of ethics than one finds in the Catholic tradition. Some, if not most, Lutherans emphasize a law–gospel dialectic where we try to live the law but cannot. Then we flee to where we are justified not by any cooperation on our own part but solely by God's declaration that we are forgiven. This could call 'ethics' into question altogether.

In an attempt to explain what a 'Lutheran ethics' might be, the 'radical Lutheran' Gerhard Forde stated, 'Put audaciously, perhaps even irresponsibly, one might announce that the problem is that Luther does not have any ethics!' For Forde, this is not a problem as much as an opportunity, for too much 'ethics' leads away from grace. What Forde means by this must be carefully nuanced if it is to be properly understood. Luther opposed the ethics of Aristotle, which he thought had become a way of salvation, especially through the basic scholastic dictum that grace did not destroy but perfect nature. For Luther, the scholastics were insufficiently radical in that they were preoccupied with an 'exodus from vice to virtue' when what was needed was one from 'virtue to grace'. For this reason, Luther spoke hyperbolically against ethics to preserve the fundamental reality that apart from grace, human creatures could do no good. But this did not mean he had no place for doing good. Forde writes, 'Ethics is not the way of salvation. It is not, to use Luther's favorite image, the tree. It is the fruit of the tree.'

Catholic and Lutheran convergence

Lutherans themselves are divided on whether Luther's position is best represented by a strong law–gospel dialectic, or by Eastern Christianity's understanding of 'theosis' or 'deification', which will be discussed below. Deification calls into question the distinction between an imputed or inherent righteousness. Because this is similar to the Roman Catholic Church's position, it provided the means by which the Roman Catholic Church and some Lutherans acknowledge their positions are not far apart in a document called 'The Joint Declaration on the Doctrine of Justification' (1999). Catholics and Protestants had been divided over the Protestant doctrine of 'justification by faith alone' since the 16th century. Catholics formulated their position against the Protestants at the Council of Trent (1545–63). The following two canons from Trent show the traditional Catholic teaching. The first canon (or teaching) suggests that the Catholics do not teach what some Protestants thought they did – justification by works.

> If anyone says that man can be justified before God by his own
> works, whether done by his own natural powers or through the
> teaching of the law, without divine grace through Jesus Christ let
> him be anathema [condemned].
>
> (Canon 1)

This second canon seemed to drive an ineradicable wedge between
Catholics and Lutherans by suggesting that the Protestants did not
have an adequate understanding of the merit of human work.

> If anyone says that the good works of the one justified are in such
> manner the gifts of God that they are not also the good merits of him
> justified; or that the one justified by the good works that he performs
> by the grace of God and the merit of Jesus Christ, whose living
> members he is, does not truly merit an increase of grace, eternal life,
> and in case he dies in grace, the attainment of eternal life itself, and
> also an increase of glory, let him be anathema.
>
> (Canon 32)

However, the 'Joint Declaration' affirmed on 31 October 1999
claims that the Protestant and Catholic positions can be
reconciled:

> Together we confess: By grace alone, in faith in Christ's saving work
> and not because of any merit on our part, we are accepted by God
> and receive the Holy Spirit, who renews our hearts while equipping
> and calling us to good works.
>
> (para. 15)

The Joint Declaration acknowledges and clarifies the perceived
differences. For instance, a Catholic understanding of our
cooperation in justification was clarified.

> When Catholics say that persons 'cooperate' in preparing for and
> accepting justification by consenting to God's justifying action, they

see such personal consent as itself an effect of grace, not as an action arising from innate human abilities.

(para. 21)

Likewise, Lutherans affirmed a proper place for human works.

We confess together that good works – a Christian life lived in faith, hope and love – follow justification and are its fruits.

(para. 37)

This Joint Declaration was historically significant, and should bear on how Christian ethics is understood in both Catholic and Protestant circles. Neither would be 'Pelagian', but nor are human works inconsequential. Ethics matters.

Catholic ethics

Catholics do not have a single, uncontested tradition about ethics. Luther's concerns about the minimal and juridical character of some Catholic ethics were not confined to Protestants alone. Servais Pinckaers, a contemporary Roman Catholic ethicist, viewed 'moral theology' undergoing a 'profound break' at the end of the Middle Ages when it produced the tradition of the 'manuals'. He credits a theology called 'nominalism' for producing the change. It so emphasized God's will that it made ethics dependent primarily upon commands. The new manuals still had an important place for the Ten Commandments and the human, divine, and natural laws, but they neglected the beatitudes and the gifts and graces of the Holy Spirit. Moral theology became decisively separate from mystical theology.

One of the results of the minimalist and juridical account of the moral life was a moral theology known as 'probabilism'. This controversial account of morality asks whether a given act is licit or illicit under the law. It does not ask whether it is virtuous; nor does it ask, as Thomas Aquinas would have, whether the act directs us towards God and the good. Instead, it seeks only to know if something is licit based on the previous precedence of at least five established authorities (at least in one version of probabilism; it has different versions). If sufficient authorities in the life of the Church affirm a certain action as licit, then that opinion can be followed.

This kind of moral theology came under attack by the Catholic Blaise Pascal (1623–62) and others, who told the story of Louis XIV who would put his mistress away on Thursday, confess to his Jesuit confessor on Friday, go to Mass on Sunday, and call her back on Monday. In his *Provincial Letters*, Pascal satirized the problems with probabilism through a conversation with a fictitious Jesuit. Pascal wrote:

> Reverend father, said I, how happy the world is in having such men as you for its masters! And what blessings are these probabilities! I never knew the reason why you took such pains to establish that a single doctor [approved teacher of the church], if a grave one, might render an opinion probable, and that the contrary might be so too, and that one may choose any side one pleases, even though he does not believe it to be the right side, and all with such a safe conscience, that the confessor who should refuse him absolution . . . would be in a state of damnation. . . . Indeed father! cried I, why on this principle the Church would approve of all the abuses which she tolerates and all the errors in all the books which she does not censure!

Probabilism 'probably' deserved such ire. It can easily produce a minimalist ethic primarily concerned with evading rules without attending to why those rules may or may not matter in the first place. Whether Pascal accurately described Jesuit practice is questionable. His own position could become so rigorous that it too lost why rules and laws might matter. Catholic ethicists can also be found who emphasize virtues, the natural law, or canon law.

Anglican ethics

The Anglican Christian ethicist Kenneth Kirk (1886–1954, Bishop of Oxford as well as Regius Professor of Moral and Pastoral Theology) suggested Christian ethics best proceeds by avoiding both formalism and rigorism. Formalism seeks to bring all of life under codification, the setting out of codes and laws that proscribe what is not to be done in advance, but actually demands very little; for all it asks is that we avoid violating some formal code. It seeks to 'discipline' through the lowest common denominator. Rigorism reacts against this formalism and demands a higher standard. But both miss something significant, suggests Kirk, and that is the 'vision of God' as the true purpose in life to which the codes or laws should be directed. For this reason, he titled his Christian ethics *The Vision of God*, and began it with a quote from the church father Irenaeus, who wrote, 'The glory of God is a living man; and the life of man is the vision of God'. Because the 'vision of God' is the 'end of life', Kirk suggested, 'the high prerogative of the Christian, in this life as well as hereafter, is the activity of *worship*; and that nowhere except in this activity will he find the key to his ethical problems'. The 'way of worship' is set against a 'formalism' or 'moralism' that becomes so preoccupied with one's own virtue or morality that it turns into a self-preoccupation; a 'vision of self' supplants the 'vision of God'. Worship re-directs us from self to God.

Orthodox ethics

The centrality of worship for ethics in Kirk's understanding of the Anglican tradition resonates well with Orthodox ethics. The Orthodox Churches of the East and the Catholic Church of the West, along with its Protestant offshoots, are sometimes distinguished by their conceptions of salvation, leading to different ethical emphases. The East supposedly focuses on salvation from death and the West from sin and guilt. The East's ethics then focus on the Incarnation and its effects on humanity, leading us into a participation in the life of God, which is called 'theosis' or 'deification' (becoming like God). The West supposedly focuses on the crucifixion and juridical accounts of atonement whereby Christ's sacrifice on the cross rids humanity of sin and guilt. But many contemporary theologians call into question any too easy distinction between them. In fact, both churches draw upon the same church fathers for their understanding of salvation, and both draw upon the sacraments, virtues, gifts, and beatitudes as central to the Christian life. This is not to deny different emphases in the two traditions.

Panayiotis Nellas, an Orthodox theologian, explains how Orthodox theology differs from the Western churches in its understandings of the human person. For the Orthodox, a 'tendency' or 'inclination' remains in the human creature after the Fall that gives a 'specific direction' towards God. This inclination is insufficient to attain God, but nor is the person so totally depraved that she or he is left with nothing by which to respond to God. Yet for Nellas, like the Catholics and the Reformed, grace alone can properly guide this inclination. He writes: 'Human nature could not have been completed simply by its tendency, it had to attain union with the Archetype.' The 'Archetype' here is Jesus, and we are originally created in his image. Therefore we have a longing or desire for union with him. After the Fall of Adam and Eve, this image is distorted. We are then given 'garments of skin' (Genesis 3:21). These 'garments' are interpreted as a 'later human nature' given to Adam and Eve, but they are not to be identified with the body. They are mortality and the concupiscent desires it brings. Although this is a judgement, it is also remedy; for they give human nature its inclination towards the Christian ethical life. God himself will be found in these same 'garments' in the Incarnation. Salvation, then, is called 'Christification' which is obtained via 'faith, keeping the commandments, ascesis, the sacraments, the whole ecclesiastical and spiritual life'. The Christian life as 'deification' or 'theosis' is an important theme in much of early Christian tradition. A. N. Williams explains ethics in terms of it:

It asserts the *imago Dei* and the Incarnation as the basis of deification and construes theosis overwhelmingly in terms of knowledge, virtue, light and glory, participation and union. In some authors, the sacraments are important tradents of divinization; more often, human faculties such as the intellect and the ability to love are significant.

This then assumes some 'degree of human striving toward virtuous assimilation to God', but love of, and union with, God always comes as a 'divine gift, a gift of grace'. Williams finds this theme present in the Western, Catholic tradition as well as the Eastern, Orthodox one.

Reformed ethics

Deification is seldom found in the Reformed tradition; its emphasis on total depravity mitigates against it. For Calvin, 'concupiscence' (the garments themselves in the Orthodox tradition) is already a sin whether one acts upon it or not. He wrote:

> ... between Augustine and us we can see that there is this difference of opinion; while he concedes that believers as long as they dwell in mortal bodies are so bound by inordinate desires that they are unable not to desire inordinately, yet he does not call this disease 'sin.' Content to designate it with the term 'weakness' he teaches that it becomes sin only when either act or consent follows the conceiving or apprehension of it, that is, when the will yields to the first strong inclination. We, on the other hand, deem it sin when man is tickled by any desire at all against the law of God. Indeed, we label 'sin' that very depravity which begets in us desires of this sort.

All are already depraved by concupiscence and the only way to overcome it is by God's election. Only as God 'elects' to redeem us by God's grace can we possibly have desires restored such that we might keep God's law. This provides a very different account of ethics than is found in the Orthodox Church. Reformed ethics tend to focus on commands God gives, which we are to obey, but can only do so if God elects us so to do.

Evangelical ethics

This remains a key influence in much of 'Evangelical' theology and its understanding of ethics, which are often based upon a 'divine command' theory, whereby God wills an action to be done and in the willing of that action also provides the grace to accomplish it. The Evangelical theologian Roger Olson states that Christian ethics for Evangelicals rests solely on revelation rather than nature. He writes:

> Evangelical ethical reflection and guidance rests on divine commands; almost all evangelical ethical thinkers appeal to commands of God found in Scripture as ultimate norms, even if they also seek to demonstrate their rationality and ethical flexibility and fruitfulness for normal human living.

Even those good works accomplished outside the Church are acts of grace, often referred to as 'common grace'.

Anabaptist ethics

In the 16th century, Protestants and Catholics could not agree on much. One thing they did agree on was their opposition, often violent, to the 'Anabaptists'. Since this Christian community did not believe Christians should use violence, violent opposition to them was easy. Their enemies called them 'Anabaptists', which means 're-baptizers'. They are also known as the 'radical wing' of the Reformation. They did not arise from a single reformer or place, but from several of both. They became known for their own specific take on the marks of the church: adult baptism, the ban, the common Supper, and 'mutual aid'. Eventually, they also became known for a 'common purse', whereby they shared goods in common; non-violence; and the practice of 'binding and loosing'. The practice of the 'ban' to resolve disputes comes from Matthew 18:15–20 and seeks restoration by first going to an offender and confronting him or her. If this is to no avail, then you take someone else along to help effect restoration. If this remains ineffectual, then the offended tells the matter to the Church and the offender is placed under the 'ban' whereby they are considered outside the community, in need of restoration.

The Anabaptist practice of binding and loosing is one way the Church disciplines its members. It differs from Catholic forms where the bishops, and above all the Bishop of Rome, are given the 'keys to the kingdom' in order to determine what is permitted and what is prohibited. The biblical warrant for this tradition is Matthew 16:18–19, in which Jesus gives the keys to the kingdom to Peter, who first confesses he is the Messiah. Jesus says:

> You are Peter and on this rock I will build my church and the gates of Hades will not prevail against it. I will give you the keys to the kingdom of heaven and whatever you bind on earth will be bound in heaven and whatever you loose on earth will be loosed in heaven.

This is why the symbol of the papacy is two keys (Illustration 7).

Summary

This brief history of the origin and execution of Christian ethics within the Church shows that it is both for and against 'ethics'. It is for ethics in that what humans do matters. Most Christian traditions agree that all humans are capable of ethical action. In fact, Pierre Bayle (1647–1706), a Christian philosopher, stated that a society of atheists could be ethical. A similar argument was debated among the Spanish scholastics of the 16th and 17th centuries with the 'discovery' of the Native Americans. While some, such as Sepúlveda, argued that they were natural slaves and could not be trusted to form good societies, the majority opinion was the opposite. God had so created the world that good could be found among its various nations, even those who did not know God. But Christian ethics

7. The two keys represent the two keys Jesus gives to Peter. Roman Catholics understand this as giving the Bishop of Rome, the Pope, the power to exercise authority in the Church

is also against ethics because something more than our own nature is necessary. For the good to be truly attained, nature is presupposed and perfected but may also need to be disrupted and corrected.

The second section: '. . . for the sake of the nations'

To this point, we examined Christian ethics internal to the Church and its calling 'not to be like the other nations'. The first context for Christian ethics is the community of faith as it seeks to embody the life to which God calls. But it is also called to do this for the sake of the nations. How it has fulfilled and failed to fulfil that task is also a crucial element in the history of Christian ethics. The failure to fulfil this mission was a central cause in Christ's crucifixion.

We have no king but Caesar

In his trial, Jesus is brought before the Roman prefect Pilate, who asks the Jewish elders, 'Shall I crucify your King?' To which the chief priests answer, 'We have no king but Caesar' (John 19:15). Anyone who has followed the biblical narrative to this point would let out an audible gasp; the Gospel here is intentionally provocative. The chief priests betrayed the call of Abraham 'not to be like the other nations'. Yahweh alone was to be king. In order to deliver Jesus to death, the chief priests betray him and their own history by calling on the security of Rome. The New Testament scholar Raymond Brown suggests that this may give us authentic historical insight as to the reason Jesus was crucified – worry about what they would say in Rome.

This is a constant temptation not only for Israel but also for the Church. The temptation takes diverse forms. At times, the king or governing authority gets treated as divine or as head of the Church. This is called 'Caesaropapism'. At other times, bishops or leaders of the Church act more like kings than Christ's ministers. Still another version of this temptation is to turn the Church into a 'chaplain' to the state, whereby it seeks only to do its bidding. We will discuss below various historical failures – crusade, conquests, inquisitions – that arose from these failures. They are often temptations for the Church to resemble the power of the state.

Walter Miller's novel *Canticle for Leibowitz* explains the temptation to Caesaropapism. After a number of unfortunate incidents, newly formed states engage in battle with nuclear weapons, threatening the earth itself. A character in the narrative, the abbot of a monastery, surveys the damage and comments on how such devastation arose:

Always culminates in the colossus of the State, somehow, drawing about itself the mantle of godhood, being struck down by wrath of Heaven. Why? We shouted it loudly enough – God's to be obeyed by nations as by men. Caesar's to be God's policeman, not His plenipotentiary successor, nor His heir. To all ages, all people – 'Whoever exalts a race or a State or a particular form of State or the depositories of power . . . whoever raises these notions above their standard value and divinizes them to an idolatrous level, distorts and perverts an order of the world planned and created by God . . . ' Where had that come from? Eleventh Pius, he thought. But when Caesar got the means to destroy the world, wasn't he already divinized? Only by the consent of the people – same rabble that shouted: *'Non habemus regem nisi caesarem'* [we have no king but Caesar] when confronted by Him – God Incarnate, mocked and spat upon. Caesar's divinity is showing itself again.

From popes to Protestants, traditionalists to Reformers to revisionists, a perennial temptation is to dissolve the form of God's people into 'the nations'. The temptation is to say, 'we have no king but Caesar'.

This is not to argue that the nations, the 'state', or social institutions other than the Church are somehow intrinsically evil, from which Christian ethics demands withdrawal. Quite the contrary! All their goodness has a place in God's kingdom (Revelation 21:26). The purpose of Christian ethics is to fashion the people of God in order to serve the 'nations'. This has been accomplished through a variety of means in Christian tradition. We will examine some of the most important of them.

Relating to the nations

One of the first articulations as to how Christians should relate to other peoples or nations is found in the Epistle to Diognetus, perhaps a late 2nd-century document. It tells us that Christians are not distinguished from others 'by country, nor language, nor the customs which they observe'. In other words, the Christian vocation is not to create its own country, language, or custom apart from others. The epistle continues:

> But, inhabiting Greek as well as barbarian cities, according as the lot of each of them has determined, and following the customs of the natives in respect to clothing, food, and the rest of their ordinary conduct, [Christians] display to us their wonderful and confessedly striking method of life. They dwell in their own countries, but simply as sojourners. As citizens, they share in all things with others, and yet endure all things as if foreigners. Every foreign land is to them as their native country, and every land of their birth as a land of strangers. They marry, as do all [others]; they beget children; but they do not destroy their offspring. They have a common table, but not a common bed. They are in the flesh, but they do not live after the flesh. They pass their days on earth, but they are citizens of heaven.

The epistle to Diognetus sets forth a tension always present in Christian ethics. On the one hand, Christians find 'every foreign land' amenable as a place in which they can live and 'share in all things with others', including their understanding and pursuit of the good. On the other, every land, even their native one, is to be to them a 'land of strangers' where they 'endure all things as if foreigners'. Can such a tension provide a workable ethic?

This tension produced varying results in how Christians live among the nations. For instance, both Origen and Tertullian denied that Christians should serve in public office or in the military of those nations in which they found themselves. Such positions did not serve the 'good' to be preserved, but this did not mean they denied cooperation and solidarity in other matters. For instance, Tertullian wrote:

> But we are called to account as harm-doers on another ground, and are accused of being useless in the affairs of life. How in all the world can that be the case with people who are living among you, eating

72

the same food, wearing the same attire, having the same habits, under the same necessities of existence? We are not Indian Brahmins or Gymnosophists, who dwell in woods and exile themselves from ordinary human life. We do not forget the debt of gratitude we owe to God, our Lord and Creator; we reject no creature of His hands, though certainly we exercise restraint upon ourselves, lest of any gift of His we make an immoderate or sinful use. So we sojourn with you in the world, abjuring neither forum, nor shambles, nor bath, nor booth, nor workshop, nor inn, nor weekly market, nor any other places of commerce. We sail with you, and fight with you, and till the ground with you; and in like manner we unite with you in your traffickings – even in the various arts we make public property of our works for your benefit. How it is we seem useless in our ordinary business, living with you and by you as we do, I am not able to understand.

Exactly what Tertullian meant here by we 'fight with you' is unclear, for in other statements he made clear that Christians could not participate in warfare, for when Christ took away the sword from Peter on the night of his arrest, he took it away from all Christians.

By the time we get to St Augustine (354–430), things have shifted somewhat. He too preserves the tension we find in the Epistle to Diognetus, and argues that Christ is the only source of virtue for a truly just society because he rescues us from the deep problem in every political society, which is the fact that 'the lie' primarily constitutes our social relations. The Church makes possible social bonds, unlike the Roman Empire, that do not depend upon deceit. But even for Augustine, this does not mean Christians abandon Rome. They cooperate as much as they can, pursuing a common peace, with proper worship discriminating what is and is not possible. Augustine writes:

> The heavenly city, while it sojourns on earth . . . not scrupling about diversities in the manners, laws, and institutions whereby earthly

peace is secured and maintained, but recognizing that, however various these are, they all tend to one and the same end of earthly peace. . . . [is] so far from rescinding and abolishing these diversities, that it even preserves and adopts them *so long only as no hindrance to the worship of the one supreme and true God is thus introduced.*

Even the heavenly city, therefore, while in its state of pilgrimage, avails itself of the peace of earth, and . . . desires and maintains a common agreement among men regarding the acquisition of the necessities of life *so far as it can without injuring faith and godliness.*

For Augustine, worship and holiness qualifies the relation between the two cities.

The tension certainly collapses when emperors adopt Christianity and begin to act like bishops, thinking their task is to create and enforce Christian doctrine and ethics. When this happens, the task of the Church is to remind the ruling authority of his limited role. An ancient saying of the Church captured this – 'if you want a Theodosius, you need an Ambrose'. Theodosius was emperor from 378 to 392. Ambrose was bishop of Milan. After a Christian uprising that resulted in monks and the local bishop burning down a Jewish synagogue in Thessalonika, Theodosius responded by requiring the bishop to rebuild the synagogue. Then one year later, the people of Thessalonika rebelled against Theodosius's army officer. Theodosius responded violently; his army slaughtered seven thousand people. Ambrose responded by telling Theodosius he could not come to the Eucharist because he had blood on his hands. The result was that Theodosius agreed and did penance. As David Bentley Hart argues, this was a mixed incident. On the one hand, it desacralized the state. It could never again claim divinity without challenge. On the other, it produced the 'unhappy marriage of church and state' that has haunted Western politics since. Antonis van Dyck made a famous painting of this incident, dramatizing it by making Ambrose confront Theodosius at the

8. Saint Ambrose confronting the emperor Theodosius. This story became the basis for one understanding of the relation

door of the church (Illustration 8). The event was not that dramatic, no confrontation occurred at the door of the church, but Ambrose did send a letter to Theodosius, confronting his violence and telling him that he could not say Mass in his presence.

Despite its legendary accretions, and ambiguous morality, this incident between Theodosius and Ambrose nonetheless sets forth an important theme in Christian tradition as to how it serves the nations. Christianity has a long tradition of reminding the ruling authorities of their limits, even when the Church's leaders begin to resemble those ruling authorities. There was Tertullian, who told the emperor 'look behind you, you are but a man'; Maximus the Confessor (580–662), whose tongue was cut out and hand cut off for reminding the emperor that he was no priest; St Francis of Asissi (1181–1226), who challenged the Church's complicity with the wealthy and powerful; Catherine of Siena (1347–80), who sought the peace of the Church when it was divided against itself; Peter Chelcicky (1390–1460), who told pope and emperor that their union of power was inconsistent with following Christ; Thomas More (1478–1535), who refused to recognize Henry VIII's act of supremacy by which he claimed authority over the Church; Bartolomé de las Casas (1484–1566), who challenged the Spanish conquerors of the Americas; Martin Luther (1483–1546), who called into question the papacy's temporal authority over a military crusade; Dorothy Day (1897–1980), who said the US president 'Truman' was no 'true man' for violating the Church's teaching on war by the bombing of Nagasaki and Hiroshima; Dietrich Bonhoeffer (1906–45), who refused participation with Hitler's usurpation of the Church and paid for it with his life; Martin Luther King (1929–68), who reminded the governing authorities that an 'unjust law was no law at all' in the context of laws demanding segregation of whites from blacks; Oscar Romero (1917–80), who commanded El Salvadoran soldiers to put down their weapons during the repression against the poor. These are, of course, only a few Christian witnesses who reminded emperors, popes, mayors, presidents, and others of the way of Christ. They are not all unambiguous saints, but, like Ambrose, they served the 'nations' by reminding them of their role in God's economy. In so doing, they help us understand Jesus's opaque words, 'Render to Caesar the things that are Caesar's and to God the things that are God's' (Matthew 22:21).

Serving the nations

Christian ethics serves the nations by reminding government of its limits, but it also makes important positive contributions. It should affirm what is good in every culture, working in cooperation with it. Christian ethics follows local customs, cultivates common habits, and avails itself of earthly peace (to cite again the Epistle to Diognetus, Tertullian, and Augustine). For instance, Christian ethics affirms, preserves, and turns into international law, the Roman Cicero's teaching on the just war (about which more will be said below). At the same time, it questions war's appropriateness for a creation made good by God, and constantly asks whether Christians are called to pacifism. Likewise, it affirms our possessions are to be held in service to a common good, even while it has a longstanding affirmation of private property within proper limits. It also has a tradition of holding goods in common, a form of Christian socialism.

Christian ethics makes common cause with similar ethics wherever they can be found. The goodness of God's creation, and the confession that all things are made through Christ, means that Christians are not surprised when they find his way of life vindicated in creation apart from those who explicitly confess him. Some call this 'natural law', others 'common grace'. The Anabaptist theologian John Howard Yoder suggested it revealed the deep Christological structure to God's good created order. He wrote: 'People who bear crosses are working with the grain of the universe.' For Yoder, Christian discipleship, including the refusal to use violence, can be found in and outside the Church because God who creates all things is the same God who discloses himself in Christ, redeeming the world. Christ's life remains normative, even when it finds expression in creation outside the Church. Even those Christian ethicists who affirm a natural law based on self-preservation that requires, or at least permits, the use of violence within certain limits would have to agree that Christ's life remains normative.

Notice, for instance, the following report on Benedict XVI's praise for the non-violent work of youth in the Italian Civil Service. Benedict stated:

> the authentic conversion of hearts represents the right way, the only way that can lead each one of us and all humanity to the peace that we hope for. It is the way indicated by Jesus: He – the King of the universe – did not come to bring peace to the world with an army, but through refusing violence [which is the way] followed not only by the disciples of Christ, but by many men and women of good will, courageous witnesses of non-violence. [We] cannot fail to praise those who renounce the use of violence in the vindication of their rights and who resort to methods of defense which are otherwise available to weaker parties too, provided this can be done without injury to the rights and duties of others or of the community itself.

Benedict XVI, the leader of the Roman Catholic Church, and John Howard Yoder, the influential Anabaptist theologian, do not agree completely. But they both recognize that Jesus refused violence, that his life is normative and should be affirmed when others embody it, and that such an embodiment can be found in and outside the Church. The task of Christian ethics is to affirm the mission to embody the life of Jesus in the world, and to affirm it wherever it is found. What both Yoder and Benedict share is the conviction that it is the dogmatic certainty that Jesus is who the Church professes him to be that is the basis for cultivating, discovering, and affirming the good in creation. This seems counter-intuitive, and, as we shall see, modern ethics finds it difficult to affirm, but Christian ethics suggests that it is the truth of its particular, dogmatic commitments that makes it open and welcoming to others.

Now we must return to the question of the relation between Christianity and ethics, for once again this question acutely arises. Is such a 'call' and 'mission' to the world ethical? If Christian ethics depends upon its dogmatic claims as well as the social form of the Church as the ongoing mission to fulfil the call of Abraham not to be like the other nations for the sake of the nations, does this inevitably result in failures of imperialism and colonialism? It is the missionary character of this body that worries some, especially postcolonialist thinkers who help us recognize and avoid the lingering sources of colonialism. For instance, Walter Mignolo finds that religions of the 'Book' like Christianity inevitably foster colonialism. Once you have a notion of a 'Sacred Book' that contains truth, then you get 'religions of conversion', and, citing Jack Goody, he states, 'you can spread them like jam'. Mignolo continues: 'What is important here is not the "content" of the Book but rather the very existence of the object in which a set of regulations and metaphors was inscribed, giving to it the special status of Truth and Wisdom.' If you have a Book filled with 'Truth' and 'Wisdom', which is considered to be the Word of God, then you will have a universal standard by which you evaluate and tacitly subordinate all other cultures. Is the mission itself immoral? Should there not be an appreciation of all religions, cultures, and peoples without any hierarchical evaluation of one as truer or wiser than another, an eschewal of all dogmatic certainty? Should we seek to find a common basis for ethics that would not exclude anyone? This was the hope of modern ethics, and remains, in some form, the hope of a postcolonial ethic as well.

Chapter 3
Christian ethics in and beyond modernity

Stating precisely where a modern ethics begins is something of an arbitrary exercise. Perhaps we could begin with Luther (1483–1546), who took Aquinas to task for using Aristotle's virtue tradition. He wrote:

> Then there is Aristotle's 'Ethics', which is accounted one of the best, but no book is more directly contrary to God's will and the Christian virtues. Oh, that such books could be kept out of the reach of all Christians!

But of course Luther himself appeals here to 'Christian virtues'. He did not abandon that tradition even if he could not find a minimal place for Aristotle's virtues as Aquinas did when he called them 'virtues in the restricted sense'. Or we might begin with the true architects of what would rightly pass as modern ethics in the philosophers Immanuel Kant (1724–1804) and John Stuart Mill (1806–73). Both sought a common basis for ethics that would include all people.

Mill's ethics is similar in some ways to Aristotle's; it also sets forth happiness as our *telos*. But happiness is now understood specifically as the pursuit of pleasure and/or the diminishment of pain. Mill's utilitarian ethic summons people to pursue the greatest good for the greatest number. It fits well with what economists call 'marginalism', whereby we enter into exchanges as long as we think the exchange has a 'margin' of benefit for us. We stop when we no longer find exchanging satisfying. Kant's ethics is 'deontological', which comes from the Greek word *deontos*, which means 'binding'. Contrary to a utilitarian or Aristotelian ethic, it does not have a *telos* to which every action aims, but assumes we should do the right thing without being preoccupied with the consequences by following the categorical imperative – 'act only on that maxim which you can at the same time will to be a universal law'. A maxim is a law an individual gives herself, but it is only moral if she can also will that anyone in any circumstance would do the same.

What is interesting about the development of these modern ethics is how the social context for the pursuit of the good changed. Plato and Aristotle's virtue tradition assumed that context was the city. Augustine and Aquinas assumed it was the Church. For Mill, the context has shifted to that of the market; he worked for one of the first transnational corporations, the British East India Company. Kant's ethics can best be understood within the dual context of the modern nation-state and an emerging internationalism or 'cosmopolitanism'. It comes as no surprise, then, that Mill offers us a utilitarian ethic and Kant a deontological one, for both of these ethics fit well with such social contexts.

Ethics for the modern nation

Two important contemporary political theorists, John Rawls and Jürgen Habermas, develop a Kantian ethic for democratic nations. For Rawls, like Habermas, justice is a virtue independent of theological virtues. Therefore it allows every individual to abstract from her or his religious commitments and join together in a reasonable consensus without any overarching religious or metaphysical end that binds them together. This consensus does not necessarily contradict religious commitments, but they are understood primarily as private or non-public forms of reason. Habermas developed Kant's thought in terms of the communal character of rationality. Reason is located neither in individual subjectivity nor in the cosmos, but in the pragmatic interactions among people. This functions as a pragmatic *telos* that does not emerge from some source other than interpersonal communication. For both Rawls and Habermas, politics emerges as an autonomous act of persons who come together in consensual acts. It is not produced from outside itself. It is in no sense a super-natural gift bestowed and received. God may be permitted, but is in no sense necessary for a true and good politics.

This Kantian ethics and its political correlate seeks to build solidarity among people who do not share a common *telos* other than that of their own making. Modern ethics emerges when people no longer assume a common, transcendent good that pulls all desires towards it. Modern ethics might best be understood as either an acknowledgement that no such end exists or as a revolt against it. Much of this has to do with the transition from an Aristotelian science to a modern understanding that occurred during the famous Galileo affair. In one sense, the world became 'unhinged' from the sun. We no longer think of ourselves as living in a fixed, stable universe with the earth and humanity at its centre and everything revolving around it. There is no single axis that orients the moral life. We have no 'cardinal' virtues. Moderns know everything 'moves', including people's understanding of 'the good'. In fact, it moves in infinite directions, which we see outwardly through our telescopes and inwardly through our microscopes. In such a vast, moving expanse, many persons no longer find arguments for '*the* good' persuasive. This is both our promise and our dilemma.

The promise is an end to the 'unhappy marriage' between the Church and Western political structures. The dilemma is that no account of the good, including the Christian one, now has a universal hold. Perhaps the result will be that the good becomes 'nothing', and we lose the ability to speak of 'the good' at all; the result is 'nihilism' – we are on a little blue ball spinning through space with no purpose or direction. Even if someone finds this objectionable, few would affirm that Christian faith shows us 'the good'. Such a claim is readily countered by others who would list its many failures: crusades, conquest, slavery, inquisitions, and the Galileo affair, which do not of course constitute an exhaustive list. Doesn't a modern ethics emerge because of the failure of Christian claims to goodness and truth? Perhaps, although careful study of this history would show it is more ambiguous than is popularly recognized.

Crusading and other Christian failures

The Crusades were a particular failure, both theologically and politically. They were considered just wars, which were fought to liberate the Holy Land from Islamic conquest. They began in 1095 as pilgrimages and were often undertaken as acts of penance. Crusaders were granted indulgences and possibly the state of martyrdom. They were life-consuming activities that required long journeys and a near-ascetic existence. Sometimes crusading parties never made it to the Holy Land but fought other Christians for provisions and territory. When a second series of Crusades were launched between 1204 and 1291, a century of crusading had already taken its toll. The Crusades soon lost popularity. They were expensive, time-consuming, and dangerous. Increased efforts to promote them were required by the Church and the secular leaders, since they were now primarily for the purposes of defending Christian territories.

The crusading practices developed over three centuries were soon directed at the so-called 'New World'. In 1492, Columbus set sail for the Indies and stated to King Ferdinand and Queen Isabella that his intention was to finance another crusade. He wrote: 'I declared to Your Highnesses that all the gain of this my enterprise should be spent in the conquest of Jerusalem.' However,

Jerusalem became less a concern than the New World. The result was the 'great dying' during which millions lost their lives, some from slaughter but the vast majority from slavery or abysmal working conditions. Malnutrition and diseases like smallpox and measles were deadly under such conditions.

There were voices of resistance (Illustration 9). Bartolomé de las Casas reported the following sermon, supported by his Dominican brothers, by Friar Antón Montesino against those who perpetrated such atrocities:

> You are all in mortal sin! You live in it and you die in it! Why? Because of the cruelty and tyranny you use with these innocent people. Tell me, with what right, with what justice, do you hold these Indians in such cruel and horrible servitude? On what authority have you waged such detestable wars on these people, in their mild, peaceful lands, where you have consumed such infinitudes of them, wreaking upon them this death and unheard of havoc?.... Are you not obliged to love them as you love yourselves? Do you not understand this? Do you not grasp this? How is it that you sleep so soundly, so lethargically? Know for a certainty that in the state in which you are you can no more be saved than Moors or Turks who have not, nor wish to have, the faith of Jesus Christ.

Las Casas himself gave a 'Defence of the Indians' which led to a debate at Valladolid in Spain in 1550. Juan Ginés de Sepúlveda (1494–1573) debated with Las Casas on the legitimacy of the conquest. Sepúlveda, drawing on Aristotle's argument that some persons are naturally inferior, argued that the Native Americans should be colonized because the natural law requires inferior persons to obey 'those who are outstanding in virtue and character'. Las Casas disagreed, arguing that the Spaniards committing these atrocities were more 'barbarian' than the Indians Sepúlveda demeaned. Las Casas did not find Sepúlveda's use of Aristotle's natural law consistent with Scripture. Thus he states, 'Good-bye, Aristotle! From Christ, the eternal truth, we have the

9. Diego Rivera's mural showing Bartolomé de las Casas setting himself, and the cross, between the powerful conquistadors and the poor 'pagans' they oppressed

command, "You must love your neighbour as yourself"''. Las Casas goes so far as to say, 'if preachers are accompanied by the clatter of arms when they go forth to announce the gospel to any people, by that very fact they are unworthy to have their words believed'. Neither Las Casas nor Sepúlveda won the day. Francisco de

Vitoria's work on the natural law gave the definitive argument for and against the Conquest. Only those crimes against the natural law such as human sacrifice could be a legitimate cause for Spanish interference in the lives of others.

Slavery

The crusading and colonizing practices from the 11th through to the 16th centuries continued in the development of new forms of slavery. Slavery itself was nothing new. It had been present long before Judaism and Christianity. Judaism had regulations to mitigate its harsh reality, since the Jews recognized themselves as slaves in Egypt. In fact, the concern for the poor and oppressed largely enters Western culture through Judaism and Christianity. In the Jubilee year, as Leviticus 25 stipulates, slaves were to be set free. The end of slavery was associated with the messianic vision, the time when God would restore creation to God's intended purposes. This vision may very well be one of the inaugurating events of Jesus's ministry in Luke 4: 'He has sent me to proclaim release to the captives.' Christianity, however, did not originally rule out slavery, even though the apostle Paul taught that in Christ there were neither free nor slave, which was associated with a new status brought about by baptism:

> As many of you as were baptized into Christ have clothed yourselves
> with Christ. There is no longer Jew or Greek, there is no longer
> slave or free, there is no longer male and female; for all of you are
> one in Christ Jesus. (Galatians 3:27–9)

But this promise would take a long time to come to fruition. In fact, Paul sends the emancipated slave Onesimus back to his master Philemon. Although Paul explicitly states that Philemon is to receive Onesimus 'no longer as a slave, but more than a slave, a beloved brother' (Philemon v. 16). As Oliver O'Donovan put it:

The early church, often criticized for failing to demand the 'abolition' of slavery, dealt with the institution in the most direct way: it treated the proprietorial idea as fraudulent mystification; it taught its slave-members to regard their 'masters' as brothers who depended on their help. When a true description of the relation was in place, the legal construct could only lose its credibility.

What the Church critiqued is the false and impossible assumption that someone can ever own another person's labour. This is impossible, O'Donovan argues, because 'Divine providence never allows two human beings to work together without discovering some kind of community.'

Yet it is the case that only a few early Christian fathers and mothers, such as Gregory of Nyssa and Maximus the Confessor, explicitly denounced the evils of slavery. Most theologians, from Augustine to Las Casas, linked slavery and war. They were linked by the rights victors had against the conquered. As Gustavo Gutiérrez notes, 'the victims in a just war . . . had a right to enslave the vanquished. To make them slaves for life instead was regarded as a concession, almost a humanitarian gesture.' Slavery was legal during much of the Conquest as long as its victims were captured in a legitimate just war. This would shift in the North American slavocracy where a new legitimation arose for it based on the modern scientific category of race. Here, a peculiar understanding of the Bible, coupled with a peculiar understanding of science, came together to justify black slavery on the basis of racial superiority and inferiority. But the enslavement of black Africans occurred long before this; it was a legitimation after the fact.

Not until the late 18th century did Christians and others begin to see how incompatible slavery was with the Gospel. But it was primarily Christians who recognized this against other Christians. Some of these Christians were of African descent and had themselves been slaves. They recognized the incompatibility long before others, and took bold and courageous steps to present it in all its horrible truth.

Jarena Lee was born into slavery in 1783, taken from her parents at the age of seven, and called to preach in 1804. She claimed the right to preach because of the example of the Virgin Mary who first made Jesus present. In Jarena Lee's preaching, she forgave all who harmed her. Her presence was so powerful that it converted slaveholders from their previous false understanding. For instance, a Deist slaveholder attended one of her sermons out of curiosity. He did not believe Africans had souls (a position rejected by the Catholic Church since the debates at Valladolid). But her preaching was so persuasive he had to recognize his previous errors. Lee recounts the story:

> After I had done speaking, he went out, and called the people around him, said that my preaching might seem a small thing, yet he believed I had the worth of souls at heart. This language was different from what it was a little time before, as he now seemed to admit that coloured people had souls, as it was to these I was chiefly speaking; and unless they had souls, whose good I had in view, his remark must have been without meaning. . . . This man was a great slave holder, and had been very cruel, thinking nothing of knocking down a slave with a fence stake, or whatever might come to hand. From this time it was said of him that he became greatly altered in his ways for the better.

This may seem like a small witness. The slaveholder did not give up his slaves. Lee was not Harriet Tubman (1820–1913) who ran missions for the Underground Railroad. Nor did she try to lead a revolt against slavery like John Brown (1800–59), a conservative, evangelical Calvinist, who found the pacifism of many abolitionists distasteful and started an insurrection against slavery at Harper's Ferry, Virginia. He was tried and hung for it. But the 'small thing' her preaching represented produced a conversion in the culture that would make good on the vision early Christians such as Gregory of Nyssa and Maximus the Confessor recognized.

Inquisitions

In comparison to the Crusades, the Conquest, and slavery, the Inquisition and the Galileo affair are minor failures, but failures nonetheless. The Spanish Inquisition is inseparable from Christian persecution of Jews. Although persecuted in Spain in the 7th century, Jews lived alongside Christians and Muslims in Spain during the Middle Ages in what is known as a time of '*convivencia*'. Of course, historians are divided on how peaceful these relations were, but they were certainly better than what occurred once the Spanish Inquisition began investigating the '*conversos*' (Jewish converts to Christianity) in the 15th century. In fact, at the Council of Arles, France, in 1235, it was decided that Jews throughout Europe were required to wear a yellow patch. Spain refused.

The process of 'inquisition' was known prior to the Spanish Inquisition. It had a long history. Throughout the Middle Ages, it was the office charged with ensuring orthodoxy. In 1542, Pope Paul III transformed it into the 'Congregation of the Holy Office'. It was the 'Holy Office', or 'Inquisition', that tried Galileo and found him guilty of 'vehement suspicion of heresy' – a specific, legal charge that was actually less than the committee's report against him, the greater charge of 'formal heresy'.

The Spanish Inquisition, however, may be the most infamous of all the inquisitions. It was an odd mix of Church and secular authority. It was primarily instituted, however, not by the Church, but by secular authority. In fact, the Holy Office questioned its authority several times during its existence. King Ferdinand of Aragon instituted it in order to help solidify the religious unity of Spain. The Inquisition had authority only over Christians. In Spain, Jews, Christians, and Muslims lived together, but in 1492, Jews were required to be baptized or to leave Spain. Once they were baptized, then they came under the authority of the Inquisition. Although a number of theologians and Church leaders raised questions about the legitimacy of such forced baptisms, the majority defended these practices on the basis that the Jewish converts were baptized voluntarily because they had the option of exile. The vast majority of Jews did 'convert', although it is no surprise that such conversions were in name only. Many continued Jewish practices, which is where the Spanish Inquisition stepped in. It was instituted to test the legitimacy, primarily, of the *conversos*' faith. The primary charge punished under the Spanish Inquisition was 'judaizing' – continuing Jewish practices, although other charges were also brought, including witchcraft. These inquisitorial practices against *conversos* were later implemented against Muslims, who were known as 'Moriscos'. The Spanish crown certainly used the Church to implement these policies.

Galileo (1564–1642) became convinced by the scientific work of the Polish Christian priest Nicolaus Copernicus (1473–1543). His calculations suggested that the movement of the planets assumed by the Ptolemaic system, whereby the earth was thought to be the centre of the universe and the sun moved around it, could equally be explained if the sun were the centre and the earth was a planet that revolved around it. Copernicus's ideas were well known long before the Galileo affair began in 1613 and had not created controversy. Galileo refined the telescope, and with it, he began affirming Copernicus's theory from hypothesis to fact. In 1613, he was told by the Holy Office not to teach this as fact but as a hypothesis. However, Galileo continued to publish works that did more than present it as a hypothesis, and he attempted to defend his theory in terms of Bible and theology. Galileo argued against a 'literal' interpretation, which of course was not new. Christianity, like Judaism, had never thought that a text had only one meaning, found in the literal interpretation alone. (Only modern fundamentalists teach that type of understanding of Scripture.)

In fact, Galileo cited St Augustine extensively to make his case. However, Galileo's apology for Scripture sounded too Protestant for the Holy Office, which was then confronting what it perceived to be the Protestant understanding of the Bible – that each individual should read and interpret the text for him- or herself and not solely in terms of the tradition of interpretation of the church fathers. In 1633, Galileo was found guilty of 'vehement suspicion of heresy' and ordered under house arrest. The committee assessing Galileo's case came to two specific conclusions. First, 'That the sun is the centre of the world and motionless is a proposition which is philosophically absurd and false, and formally heretical for being explicitly contrary to Holy Scripture.' The Holy Office did not completely accept this since it did not charge him with 'formal heresy'. Second, 'That the earth is neither the centre of the world nor motionless but moves even with diurnal motion is philosophically equally absurd and false and theologically at least erroneous in the Faith.' Galileo was placed under house arrest at his villa, where he continued as a practising Catholic, regularly attending Mass.

Making sense of failure

How are we to make sense of these events, and other failures such as the Jewish Holocaust of the 20th century? Reading these histories causes bafflement. How could any person cleave open the skull of another human being while crying out 'Jesus is Lord', or put someone on the rack and watch her writhe in pain and then read the Sermon on the Mount? For some, this history is too much. The failures of Christianity to stand against these practices, let alone to be so complicit in them, gives grounds for persons with an ethical conscience to reject it. At the very least, these stories require confession and repentance from Christians. This has taken and continues to take place. John Paul II asked forgiveness during a visit to Africa in 1992. He prayed:

> From this African sanctuary of black pain, we ask forgiveness of
> heaven. We pray that, henceforward, Christ's disciples may be seen
> to be entirely faithful to the observance of the commandment of
> brotherly and sisterly love left them by their Teacher. We pray that
> they may never again be the oppressors of their own brothers and
> sisters, but may seek instead to imitate the compassion of the Great
> Samaritan of the gospel in their welcome of the needy. We pray that
> the scourge of slavery and its consequences may disappear forever.

Such stories also rightly require, and have led to, important
revisions in Christianity. This is undeniable. No official Church
body still sanctions crusades, slavery, or the use of torture to
investigate heretics, witches, or sinners (a practice that is, however,
still justified by some 'civilized' secular nations against their
enemies). Most of these corrections were internal to Christianity
itself.

If we are to speak truthfully about this history, we should avoid
thinking that some anti-religious secular organization battled
against Christians to free the masses from its authoritarian rule.
Nor was it a contest between the dogmatic orthodox and liberal
free-thinkers. Many deists who were certainly not orthodox
Christians held slaves. Although some persons recount these
stories with that in mind, this sometimes distorts the history and
uses these profound failures to secure contemporary political goals.
What is ironic is that Christians first used and even 'invented' these
stories against other Christians. This occurred both by Catholics
against other Catholics, and by Protestants who wanted to portray
the Reformation as the 'liberation of the human spirit from the
fetters of darkness and superstition'. Protestants often told these
stories to gain a comparative advantage over Catholics. John Foxe
(1517–87) drew on the Inquisition as evidence for the utter
corruption of Roman Catholicism. He wrote in his *Book of Martyrs*
that practices like the Spanish Inquisition occurred, and will occur,
wherever Catholics were in the 'ascendancy'. Now secularists often
take over this Protestant polemic and use it against Protestants

themselves. Those who view themselves on the side of liberation find self-affirmation the more they paint others as ruled by 'darkness'. In so doing, they foster a politics of fear – that were it not for 'our' side, those forces would know no end to their evil devices.

Any interpretation of these events must take care to avoid a 'moralizing' that only uses these past failures in order to demonstrate 'our' moral superiority. An old adage states that the abuse of a thing does not remove its usefulness. As this is true of Christianity, so it is true of most human endeavours. The violence of the Inquisition is miniscule in comparison to the havoc wreaked by democratic nation-states in the 20th century. Often, this violence has been perpetrated in an attempt 'to make the world safe for democracy'. Seldom does this lead someone to say, 'democracy has proven itself too dangerous, let us abandon it'. Likewise, it would be foolish to saddle Marx and/or Marxism with all the failures of many of its more heinous practitioners. And it would be foolish to argue that all 'godless atheists' will produce death-camps and genocide just because some did so.

Often critics assume that the general problem that led to these failures was that religious people thought they knew the truth about God. So the remedy is thought to be to challenge, relativize, or privatize Christian truth-claims. Oddly, seldom do you hear people diagnose these failures in terms of the actual use of violence, where the obvious remedy would be for people to desist from employing violent means. Instead, we may read the history of these failures in order to question and challenge 'truth', rather than to challenge the violent exercise of power. The latter is more central to our secular politics than it ever was in the pre-modern era.

The remedy for the past alliance between dogmatic 'religious' truth and 'secular' power is to sever this alliance and relativize claims to truth. This is common among philosophers, theologians, some religious leaders, politicians, and cultural producers. It is found in popular music and learned analyses. However, as popular as this remedy may be, it has had little success in diagnosing or remedying previous or current Western (and non-Western) failures. It often assumes that if we get rid of religion, or at least police it with secular power, violence will be diminished. There were some, such as Thomas Hobbes (1588–1679), who tried to build a politics based on the rejection of God. He put more faith in the throne than the altar and thought that if we could do away with religion, or at least subordinate it to the state, we could better promote the good and avoid evil. His position was too drastic for most people in the 17th and following centuries; few people at the beginning of the modern era thought we should do away with God altogether. (Of course, the 20th century did produce a number of explicitly secular states which sought to do this. To say the least, they did not create peaceful political orders.) A better course of action was to privatize religion and allow it the freedom to flourish as an internal, spiritual reality that had salutary ethical consequences, which was the strategy of most of the great modern political thinkers such as Kant, Rousseau, Jefferson, and Franklin. Ethics will relativize claims to Christian (and other religions') truth. Ethics is supposedly public and universal; religions, like Christianity, are private.

Postmodern ethics

Modern ethics separates 'ethics' from 'God' and privileges ethics as a category greater than God. It does this through two steps. First, 'God' becomes distant and unknowable – utterly transcendent – and nevertheless the source for the possibility of ethics. God guarantees its formal possibility without affecting its material content. Second, ethics becomes the stable referent for God. What we truly know is ethics, either as duty or the pursuit of the greatest good for the greatest number. Because we know this, God becomes a hypothetical possibility. God still has a 'place' in modern ethics, but it is as a hypothesis or a private preference. This allows people who affirm God and those who do not to join together in a common, and supposedly universal, pursuit of ethics.

Postmodernity, however, calls all this into question. It challenges any stable referent. It does not necessarily deny a 'stable referent' exists; for to assert 'there is no stable referent' would simply be to replace God or nature or ethics with the security of 'nothing'. At its best, postmodern philosophers avoid this easy critique. Instead, postmodernity avoids the closure of any totalizing account of what is good and true. In this sense, postmodernity adopts the dominant modern diagnosis of our past evils as a dogmatic attachment to truth and goodness allied with political, cultural, and philosophical power. But unlike the modern remedy, it fails to offer yet another secure foundation for the good or true that will somehow overcome our past dogmatic commitments and set us on a sure footing. We cannot 'overcome' the past by the certainty of any present reality. All we can do is *turn* such certainty against itself so it does less harm. Neither God, nor nature, nor reason, nor 'nothing' can secure us. In fact, any such foundation, even the foundation that we know with certainty, a stable distinction between good and evil, will only fund further evils.

Few people go as far as the critique of ethics that one finds in a philosopher like Nietzsche (1846–1935). In his inimitable humorous style, Nietzsche offered a scathing critique of modern ethics, especially 'moral philosophy'. He suggested it was a 'soporific appliance', by which he meant it put you to sleep much like anaesthesia before surgery. Once morality lulls you into complacency, then in its name someone can cut you open, remove what is vital, and you never feel it. Nietzsche showed us the ethicist's knife. Here is his description of what is really going on in English utilitarian ethics:

> Observe, for example, the indefatigable, inevitable English
> utilitarians: how ponderously and respectably they stalk on. . . . In

the end, they all want *English* morality to be recognized as authoritative, inasmuch as mankind, or the 'general utility', or 'the happiness of the greatest number', – no! the happiness of *England* will be best served thereby.

Like the 'new' atheists, for Nietzsche, 'God is dead'. But he thinks those who think they can reject God and still cling to morality fail to see the radical nature of God's death. Because God is dead, we no longer have a direction, no 'up or down', no 'left or right'. We are spinning through an infinite nothing. We are beyond good and evil. Moralists fail to see this and replace theologians by trying to find a security and certainty in ethics that was formerly found in God.

Contesting God and ethics

If Christianity is essentially contested in modernity for the sake of ethics, 'ethics' is contested in postmodernity. We can trace the disputed relations between God and ethics in terms of the following quotes or paraphrases that set forth diverse philosophers' understanding of this relation. The first two represent the modern attempt to make a place for God that will nonetheless subordinate theology to ethics and make the latter the primary category. The next three offer radical critiques of that effort.

> Kant: 'If the freedom to be moral exists, God can be hypothesized.'
> Rousseau: 'If the moral simplicity of the heart is, God is permitted.'
> Dostoevsky: 'If God is dead, everything is permitted.'
> Nietzsche: 'Those who reject God cling all the more firmly to ethics.'
> Žižek: 'If God is, everything is permitted.'

Kant and Rousseau represent positions furthest from Dostoevsky and Nietzsche. Kant is convinced that humans have the ability to be moral because of their freedom, but he does not know how to account for that freedom without God. God now functions as a possible ground for my freedom to be moral, which must exercise itself independently of that ground. Rousseau represents a modern/postmodern sentiment that we can have spirituality without religion. He tells a story of a Savoyard priest who once believed the truth of Christian doctrine, but gradually lost faith in its content. This did not result in the loss of faith, but its revision. True religion is the 'simplicity' (or authenticity) of a heart seeking to do good; all the dogmas, rituals, religious institutions, laws, and sacraments merely obfuscate this true religion. God remains, but is incorporated into the inner callings of such a sentimental impulse. Both of these first two approaches make the nation-state the primary context for the pursuit of ethics.

Dostoevsky never actually penned these words for which he is famous. They represent a sentiment expressed in his novel *The Brothers Karamazov*. If we lose God, if we lose immortality and transcendence, then we will lose what makes life worth living – love, goodness, truth. We will lose the quest for a mystery that is more than us, and be forced to be satisfied with a good of our own making. In this sense, Nietzsche's quotation, which seems furthest from Dostoevsky, may actually be the closest. Without God, we do not lose ethics, but we cling all the more firmly to it, even when we recognize we ourselves produce it. We must cling to it because it is all we have. We have no festivals of atonement that can redeem and forgive us for our transgressions. We only have ethics. For Nietzsche, this is a failure of nerve.

Žižek's quote poses an interesting challenge to the relation between God and ethics. Unlike Kant and Rousseau, who re-symbolize Christianity in order to make it fit modern ethics, Žižek is more akin to Hobbes or Nietzsche who thought 'God' was positively dangerous to a proper ethic. Prior to 9/11, Žižek (somewhat) defended the legacy of Christianity in a work subtitled with the question 'why is the Christian legacy worth fighting for?' After 9/11, he shifted (somewhat) and explained why the Western legacy of atheism is worth fighting for. He too refers to Christianity's failures, and writes:

During the Seventh Crusade, led by St. Louis, Yves le Breton reported how he once encountered an old woman who wandered down the street with a dish full of fire in her right hand and a bowl full of water in her left hand. Asked why she carried the two bowls, she answered that with the fire she would burn up Paradise until nothing remained of it, and with the water she would put out the fires of Hell until nothing remained of them: 'Because I want no one to do good in order to receive the reward of Paradise, or from fear of Hell; but solely out of love for God.' Today, this properly Christian ethical stance survives mostly in atheism. Fundamentalists do what they perceive as good deeds in order to fulfill God's will and to earn salvation; atheists do them simply because it is the right thing to do. Is this also not our most elementary experience of morality?

Žižek finds atheism to be the true Christian legacy. Atheists, who neither blaspheme nor condone Islamic religious practices, can treat Muslims as ethical agents by refusing to censure caricatures of Mohammed in newspapers. They do this without concern for 'God', but only concern to say what everyone knows is right – such caricatures should not result in riot and death, which occur, he suggests, when God is involved. For then we have 'permission', permission to transgress the basic civility of everyday life in the name of the God who asks it of us.

Is God the basis for ethics? If so, in what sense? Dostoevsky's? Kant's? Rousseau's? Are we better off without God at all? Are atheists now the true practitioners of Christian ethics, as Žižek suggests? That a generic, theistic conception of a god is necessary for ethics is not consistent with Christian tradition. This is why the early Christians were accused of atheism. They did not find the 'gods' of antiquity as supporting a proper way of life. In fact, they buried those gods. If they existed, they were malevolent forces. Those gods permitted horrible atrocities; no one should bow a knee to them. Modern and postmodern conceptions of 'god' often retrieve such pagan deities. We seek Thor who christens battleships and blesses the violence of torture or abortion.

Or perhaps we resurrect Dionysius, the god Nietzsche recommended against Christianity, a god who affirms the indulgence of every sensual appetite, much as the global market encourages us to do as well. Or perhaps we are satisfied with an utterly unknown god; one who never makes demands on us that violate our duty or sentiments? It is better for such gods to die; ethics cannot be had while serving them. The proper answer to the question 'is God the basis for ethics?' requires we become clearer on which God we mean, and that is not easy. For how do we know God and what God demands of us?

Theological responses to modernity/ postmodernity

Is God the basis for ethics? Which God? How might we know a God worthy of our ethical obedience? If we cannot answer these questions, we cannot give an adequate account of 'Christian ethics'. But where do we look for knowledge of God, in 'nature' or 'culture' or Scripture? If nature or culture suffices, then we can also use those sources as the basis for our ethics as well. God might be useful, but unnecessary. But if we think that 'grace', or God's gift of the Spirit to us, is necessary, then grace will have a significant role to play in our ethics as well.

The above questions arose in the 20th century because of that time's unparalleled violence. Total war, genocide, concentration camps, gulags, obliteration bombing, the atomic bomb dropped on civilian populations – all these were unprecedented in human history. The 'liberation' from Christendom into secular nation-states that marked the modern era did not end in 'Enlightenment' except the blinding fire of conflagration. This is not to argue for a return to Christendom; in many ways, it wittingly and unwittingly prepared the conditions for the rise of the secular. Perhaps religion returned, for good or ill, in our postmodern culture because secularism so obviously failed.

Two important 20th-century theological movements set the stage for the most interesting developments in Christian ethics that came as a reaction to those movements. This is surprising in that, on the surface, these two movements could not be further apart. Neo- (or liberal) Protestants embraced philosophical developments in the modern era that emphasized that all our knowledge, including that of God and the good, has been historically constructed. This made 'culture' the essential mediating norm for theology. The task of theology was to be relevant to the 'culture' as it confronted theology with new questions. Doctrine had always to be revised in correlation to the flux of history. In opposition to this, Roman Catholic theology reacted against 'modernism', even requiring an 'oath' against it. A Neoscholastic reaction against modernity and its historicism emphasized the inherent rationality of 'nature'. This preserved a sharp distinction between faith and reason, theology and philosophy, where the latter served as a necessary foundation for the former. The Neoscholastic position emphasizes metaphysics, speculative logic, and eternal truths. Liberal Protestantism emphasizes history, culture, and the 'contextual' character of all truth, claiming that we are at the 'end of metaphysics'. For the Neoprotestants, 'truth' is never conformity to 'the real', as it is with the Neoscholastics, because we have no access to the 'real', but only our perception of it, which is limited by language and culture. Nevertheless, it treats 'culture' similarly to how the Neoscholastics treat nature. Culture functions as a source for ethics that is known without the mediation of the grace. Here the Church must be relevant to its culture and accommodate it by revising basic Christian teaching in terms of the knowledge culture provides. This knowledge is not 'natural' as much as it is a 'social construction'. This assumption influences a great deal of contemporary Christian ethics, leading to the development of diverse contextual positions based on race, culture, class, gender, and sexual orientation. It has had the salutary consequence of opening up ethical reflection to persons previously under-represented, or not represented at all, in the tradition of Christian ethics. Slave narratives, women's experiences, the privileging of the poor or of other marginalized groups enrich the sources for Christian ethics. This emphasis on historicism and context also makes it more difficult to speak of a common moral good among Christians. The Neoscholastic position sees historicism compromising truth.

Two important 20th-century theologians, one Protestant and one Catholic, found significant problems in both Protestantism's accommodation of culture and Catholicism's Neoscholastic doctrine of pure nature. The Swiss Reformed theologian Karl Barth (1886–1968) and the French Jesuit Henri de Lubac (1896–1991) saw in both these seemingly opposed positions a Christian affirmation of the secular and its violence; both wrote against it. They were dissenters to both modern and Neoscholastic Christianity. Barth rejected the theology of culture found in liberal Protestantism, for he thought it blinded German theologians (including his own teachers) and Christians to see the violent political errors of the modern era. If God were primarily known through 'culture', then our knowledge of God can only affirm it. For this reason, Barth emphasized that 'grace disrupts nature'.

The Jesuit priest Henri de Lubac was a soldier in the First World War and a member of the French (spiritual) resistance in the Second. As Barth found the liberal Protestant emphasis on culture baptized the violent tendencies of his generation, de Lubac thought a Catholic doctrine of 'pure nature' caused many Catholics to compromise with Germany's occupation of France. This doctrine suggested that human creatures have a 'pure nature' independent of grace that can be known by reason alone and made the basis for ethics. This made for a moral rapprochement between those in and outside the Church, but for de Lubac it also marginalized the Church, its Sacraments, Scriptures, call to discipleship, and so on, from playing a significant ethical and political role. Like the Scholastics, he affirmed that 'grace perfects nature', but it did not perfect a nature complete in itself. It completes a nature that has a restless longing for something more; it has a 'natural desire' for God, which can only be completed by grace mediated through the Church.

What Barth and de Lubac oppose, as well as what they affirm, guides us in answering the questions noted above. Is God the basis for ethics? Which God? How might we know a God worthy of our ethical obedience? Barth critiqued correlating theology to culture for it produced a 'secular misery' that empties the Christian faith of its content and replaced it with secular conceptions of the good. Yet he did not replace 'culture' with 'nature'. Barth denied Christian ethics had the continuity natural law ethics presumed. This also had tremendous influence in Protestant Christian ethics. Taken to one extreme, it produced a position known as 'situation ethics', where only the 'situation' and nothing that comes before it provides an appropriate context for ethics. Although Joseph Fletcher, who advocated this position, saw evidence for it in Barth's work, others, such as Paul Ramsey, saw it as a caricature. Yet Barth also produced an emphasis on the doctrine of the Church as integral to a Christian ethic whereby 'witness' became a primary ethical category. The task of Christian ethics, like the image of John the Baptist in Grünewald's crucifixion (Illustration 10), is to witness to the goodness that is Jesus Christ.

For Yoder, who was influenced by Barth, Christian ethics is not finding the 'right handle' on history in order to make it come out the way one thinks it should. Instead, it is 'witnessing' to the reality that Christ inaugurates by his life, death, resurrection, and expected return. Stanley Hauerwas, also influenced by Barth, argues that Christian ethics requires a people (the Church) who embody and witness to the true and good found in the Christian 'narrative'. Hauerwas also emphasizes the habituation of the acquired virtues within the community of faith.

De Lubac influenced Christian ethics by affirming a 'single end' to which all human creatures are directed – friendship with God. This

10. Grünewald's crucifixion from the Isenheim altar. The image was central for Barth's theology. John the Baptist stands at the bottom right with the Scripture open and his finger pointing to Christ. For Barth, this is the role of Christian ethics – it is to witness, to point to what God has done for us

meant ethics cannot primarily be understood via nature alone, but requires a return to the biblical and patristic sources. De Lubac influenced the Latin American liberation theologian Gustavo Gutiérrez, as well as John Paul II and Benedict XVI. In a dialogue with Habermas on the role of Christianity in democracy, Benedict XVI (then Cardinal Joseph Ratzinger) found less help in the 'natural law' than did Habermas and wrote, 'Unfortunately, this instrument [natural law] has become blunt. Accordingly I do not intend to appeal to it for support in this conversation.' John Paul II wrote an important encyclical on moral theology called '*Veritatis Splendor*' ('The Splendour of Truth'), drawing upon the biblical story of the Rich Young Ruler (Matthew 16:19–30) to discuss ethics. He expressed concern that Catholic ethics had capitulated too much to modernity, especially through an ethics known as 'proportionalism', which argues that an act would be morally licit if it had a 'proportionate' reason, even if it should not be done otherwise. John Paul II saw this as a species of Mill's utilitarianism. In opposition to this, he emphasized that some things could never be done because they were 'intrinsically evil'; no 'proportionate reason' could ever exist for permitting such actions.

The following quote from John Paul II shows how he integrated an emphasis on 'reason' and the intelligibility of nature itself with a virtue-oriented ethic that seeks to order desire to its true ends, to the 'good of the person'. John Paul II stated:

> Reason attests that there are objects of the human act which are by their nature 'incapable of being ordered' to God, because they radically contradict the good of the person made in his image. These are the acts which, in the Church's moral tradition, have been termed 'intrinsically evil' (*intrinsece malum*): they are such *always and per se*, in other words, on account of their very object, and quite apart from the ulterior intentions of the one acting and the circumstances. . . . The Second Vatican Council itself, in discussing the respect due to the human person gives a number of examples of such acts: 'Whatever is hostile to life itself, such as any kind of homicide, genocide, abortion, euthanasia and voluntary suicide; whatever violates the integrity of the human person, such as mutilation, physical and mental torture and attempts to coerce the spirit; whatever is offensive to human dignity, such as subhuman living conditions, arbitrary imprisonment, deportation, slavery, prostitution and trafficking in women and children, degrading conditions of work which treat labourers as mere instruments of profit and not as free responsible persons.'

If we think of the various positions above in terms of a continuum, we would have at one end liberal or progressive Protestant ethics. It answers the questions of God and ethics by taking as its primary sources history and culture. At the other end would be the Neoscholastics, who take as their sources nature and reason. Barth and de Lubac come in the middle, both critiquing the dual nature of 'grace and culture' or 'grace and nature' as the best way to answer these questions. Why all this matters can be seen in our concluding section, where we look at specific issues in Christian ethics.

Chapter 4

Sex, money, and power: some questions for Christian ethics

The purpose of Christian ethics is to help us live well, and in so doing make God's Name holy. For this reason, Christian ethics deals with the most ordinary, everyday activities such as family life, sex and reproduction, economic exchange, and uses of power. Stanley Hauerwas tells of a Jewish friend who states: 'Any God who will not tell you what to do with your pots and pans and genitals isn't worth worshipping.' This is what makes Christian ethics both necessary and controversial. No one likes to be told what to do in such intimate matters; we much prefer modern autonomy. But that is not an option for Christian ethics; it must offer moral guidance on such matters, for what we do about them says something about how we hallow God's Name. It will, of course, also deal with those extraordinary events in life that people may face, such as war or abortion. But they are also always related to the ordinary.

Sex

What is the purpose of sex? The traditional Christian answer suggested three ends: unity, procreation, and fidelity. For much of Christian tradition, these three ends were united. You could not have one without being open to the others. Fidelity arises out of unity and procreation, and likewise procreation should arise from fidelity and unity. It is insufficient merely to be open to children without that openness occurring in a context of monogamous, life-long commitment. This is why Roman Catholicism teaches that the procreative end should not be artificially thwarted or the other two ends will be as well, so that marriage will be less than it could or should be. This is also why Catholicism cannot recognize divorce, although it does have casuistic means of declaring marriages annulled. For some, these positions are not only relevant to how Catholics should live, but apply to everyone because they are present in the 'nature' of sex itself.

The Orthodox Churches also have an historic opposition to birth control, but they do not have a magisterium who decides the matter. Local bishops discern what is proper in their jurisdiction. They also allow for an 'ecclesiastical divorce' followed by a second marriage that has its own liturgical rite, including a rite of penance because marriage is still assumed to be monogamous and life-long. Protestant ethics on marriage display a wide spectrum. For much of their history, Protestants also opposed artificial contraception and adhered to the traditional three ends of marriage, but this changed in the 20th century. Some still argue that procreation is a necessary feature of sexual expression, but that not every act needs to be open to children. Few Protestant Churches have any means by which to assess something like 'annulment' or 'ecclesiastical divorce'. Divorce is seldom seen as a matter for ecclesial discipline any longer.

A revisionist tradition in Protestantism renders asunder the procreative and unitive ends of marriage. It states that sex has the primary purpose of uniting two persons in an intimate relation whether they are open to conceiving children or not. Procreation is not intrinsic to the calling of marriage. These differing views obviously provide conflicting takes on the question of homosexuality. For Catholics and the Orthodox, the created *nature* of male and female is necessary for the sacrament of marriage. This too is found in the nature of things; it is a natural and metaphysical reality. Protestants are more conflicted. Once the primary purpose of sex is the intimacy of the two partners, then material natures are not as significant. Sexual expression can be understood within a changing historical context independent of 'nature'. Of course, to some extent, all Churches more or less recognize historical development in sexual practices. Scripture depicts polygamous relations as normal among the patriarchs, but no Christian Church allows for it, at least not that I know of (unless one considers very conservative Mormonism a species of Christianity). This is largely because the New Testament is the basis for the Christian reading of the Old Testament, and the unity between Christ and the Church now becomes the context for Christian marriage, making it a monogamous, life-long vocation.

Most Churches' attitudes towards homosexuality have also developed historically. Justinian's law code made gay sex a capital offence because of a bad reading of the story of Sodom and Gomorrah. Toleration of homosexual acts was thought to bring natural disasters. While one can still find this sentiment on the margins of some Christian communities, it no longer has any official standing. This is clearly a positive historical development. In addition, most Churches, including Roman Catholicism, now call into question the practice of capital punishment, another clear historical development.

Should historical development proceed to the place where homosexual relations are blessed as fulfilling the calling of marriage? This is one of the more divisive issues among Christians today. Some Churches have already decided that it should, but this is still a minority position. Where one finds oneself on the continuum between 'history' and 'nature' will have something to say about this question. If 'nature' matters, then male and female will be the material means that constitute the sacrament of marriage. If everything is fluid through its historical development, then even these natures are unstable and marriage is subject to revision. Of course, 'historicism' and 'metaphysics' are not the only two theological and philosophical contexts for discerning the question of the revision of marriage. Scripture and the virtues also play a role.

Six Scriptures in the Old and New Testaments deal in some fashion with homosexuality, although that counts the story of Sodom and Gomorrah (Genesis 19:1–29), which actually has nothing to do with homosexuality. Later Scriptures do not interpret it as 'sexual misconduct', but as is cited in Ezekiel 16:49, the 'guilt' of Sodom was 'pride, excess of food, and prosperous ease' without aiding 'the poor and needy'. The story of Sodom and Gomorrah has more to do with economics than homosexuality. Nonetheless, other passages speak to homosexuality: Leviticus 18:22, 20:13; I Corinthians 6:9–11; 1 Timothy 1:10; Acts 15:28–29; and Romans 1:18–32. Few would argue that Scripture affirms or advocates homosexuality; it obviously does not. The question is whether the contemporary understanding of the practice is the same as that which Scripture condemns. Of course, how or what it condemns still matters. The virtues of liberality and generosity move Christianity in a humanistic direction that seeks the protection and welfare of gay and lesbian individuals, who are made in the image of God, even when such unions could not be classified as 'sacramental'.

Along with the revision of marriage, another pressing issue confronting Christian ethics is new forms of human, and even 'posthuman', reproduction. Technological 'advances' make possible reproduction through artificial insemination, artificial insemination by donors, surrogacy, and even the possibility of cloning or posthuman mixing of artificial intelligence and human genetics. Obviously, for those Churches and Christians who adhere to a traditional teaching on the normativity of a married male and female couple as the context for reproduction, all of these disembodied forms of reproduction pose serious problems. No Church to my knowledge advocates for surrogacy, cloning, or posthuman reproduction. This is largely because Christians do not think it necessary for people to reproduce in order for the world to be redeemed. While some think that the only purpose to life is the continuation of the human species, even in a posthuman form, Christians cannot share that sentiment. As Paul Ramsey used to say, 'God intends to kill us all in the end'. Everyone must die. Futile or frantic efforts to secure one's life, often at the expense of others, show refusal to accept this judgement and the promise of new life in the resurrection.

This is why efforts to extend life at the expense of life, such as fetal tissue experimentation, are such important matters for Christian ethics. We do not eat our neighbours in order to satisfy our own need for protein. Nor should we create a social environment in which our health comes at the expense of others. There have been, and are, ethicists who argue that it would be licit to engineer a species of quasi-humans who could provide transplantable organs and/or labour in service to human beings, but most Christian ethicists categorically reject such a possibility (although we may nonetheless already create and/or participate in such a system by the way our daily food is produced and distributed). A more controversial question is if fetal-tissue experimentation instrumentalizes human life to serve the living at the expense of future generations. The fact that most people would object, or at least find it in extremely bad taste, to package and serve fetal tissue as human caviar to help the poor with dietary deficiencies demonstrates that most people still consider it something more than inert material like asparagus or barley. Whatever status one grants fetal tissue, it is something more than penicillin. For this reason, debates will continue to swirl around its use for experimentation.

That God intends to kill us all in the end could lead one to think that Christianity has little stake in the world as it exists. This is another charge Hitchens brought against it. It is true that Christians believe we cannot save the world through our own resources, including all the efforts at recycling and 'green energy' that we muster. Redemption comes through an 'apocalyptic' inbreaking whereby just as Christ came the first time, he will return (although no one knows exactly what that means) and inaugurate the new creation. But it is a new *creation*. This gives no licence to destroy this one. Because the good of all the nations will be preserved in the new creation, we have more rather than less reason to tend to all that is good in this one; it has eternal purpose.

Money

'Sharing' is at the heart of any Christian ethics. This could be sentimental drivel, but it is something more than that. The virtue of charity assumes that all our possessions are gifts from God with which we are entrusted, in order to serve God's creatures. We do so through *koinonia*, which means 'things held in common'. 'Socialism' was Christian before it was made 'scientific' and was fundamentally distorted by Marx and Engels. We see this in the Pentecostal miracle in Acts 2. It reverses the story of the Tower of Babel in Genesis 11. The Holy Spirit comes upon the disciples, and 'devout Jews from every nation' hear in their own language the common language of the Spirit, which produces a communion. The result is the Pentecostal miracle:

> Awe came upon everyone, because many wonders and signs were being done by the apostles. All who believed were together and had all things in common; they would sell their possessions and goods and distribute the proceeds to all as any had need.

> (Acts 2:43–45)

The miracle is that they 'had all things in common', which is a translation of the Greek word '*koinonia*'. Scripture contrasts a life in which goods are held in common (*koinonia*) with one in which each individual holds his goods only for him- or herself. This would be to hold goods as '*idion*', which is the Greek word from which the English term 'idiot' derives.

The virtues of 'justice' and 'liberality' primarily concern use of money. The vice of 'avarice' (or greed) opposes justice because it takes more profit than one is entitled to. For this reason, medieval theologians thought it proper for a destitute person to take food from someone who had abundance and was unwilling to share. This did not violate the Seventh (Eighth) Commandment not to steal. Avarice violates justice and all the virtues, especially charity. For instance, lust is a form of avarice that seeks to consume the other sexually solely for one's own pleasure, just as gluttony is greed that consumes more of one's share of 'our daily bread' than is necessary. These were not private virtues and vices; they were fundamentally public, for justice and liberality constitute a proper political economy. John Chrysostom and Thomas Aquinas cited Ezekiel 22:27 to show how such an economy goes bad: 'Her princes in the midst of her are like wolves ravening the prey to shed blood. . .and to run after gains through covetousness.'

Although only seven passages of Scripture directly address the question of homosexuality, numerous passages address the use of money. The following passages from Exodus and Luke are typical:

> If you lend money to my people, to the poor among you, you shall not deal with them as a creditor; you shall not exact interest from them. If you take your neighbour's cloak in pawn, you shall restore it before the sun goes down; for it may be your neighbour's only clothing to use as cover; in what else shall that person sleep? And if your neighbour cries out to me, I will listen, for I am compassionate.

> (Exodus 22:25–27)

> If you love those who love you, what credit is that to you? For even sinners love those who love them. If you do good to those who do good to you, what credit is that to you? For even sinners do the same. If you lend to those from whom you hope to receive what credit is that to you? Even sinners lend to sinners, to receive as much again. But love your enemies, do good, and lend, expecting nothing in

return. Your reward will be great, and you will be children of the
Most high; for he is kind to the ungrateful and the wicked. Be
merciful, just as your Father is merciful.

(Luke 6:32–36)

We should not underestimate the influence of passages such as
these on Western culture and politics. As David Bentley Hart
notes, Aristotle and much of antiquity could only conceive of a
slave economy where one's station was fixed by nature. In fact,
Christianity brings with it an understanding of the human person
that revolutionized relations between master and slave, man and
woman, parent and child. Christianity brought a 'conceptual
revolution' to a slave economy, and to the economy of men and
women and how they relate to each other, even if – as Hart also
puts it – 'the Great Church of the imperial era was not exactly
heroic in its vision of the social implications of its creed'. Economy
was not only for the purpose of gain, nor was it primarily
understood as the most efficient means to distribute scarce
resources. It was a means for exercising virtue.

But if anything has historically developed to the place where it
seems to have become a contradiction with previous eras, it is
Christian approaches to the economy. From Aristotle through
Luther, it was assumed that taking interest on money was
immoral. This was not because people lived with the false
assumption of a zero sum economy in which every profit came at
the expense of someone else; it was because money was understood
to be primarily something that facilitated equivalent exchange.
Money itself, as Aristotle put it, 'did not fructify'. That is to say,
money, unlike animals and plants, does not produce more things of
value. Profit itself was not illegitimate, but profit should occur
through a morally legitimate activity whereby goods are genuinely
increased. So, for instance, I can buy some sheep, hope they are
sufficiently randy so that they reproduce, and make a profit in
wool. I can even enter into a 'society' with others to help sell

my wool. Others can participate in my risk and my profit. What I cannot do, what was considered immoral until the rise of capitalism, was assume that my money simply made more money. Is this as foolish an idea as many modern economists suggest? (John Maynard Keynes seemed to be the sole exception.) In order to test this idea, I performed an experiment a few years back. I took two one-dollar bills, placed them in a cosy, secluded place on my desk, dimmed the lights, played some romantic Barry White music, and waited. Nothing happened. Indeed, money does not fructify.

I recognize that when we now speak as if money makes money, we do not really disagree with Aristotle and Aquinas. What we mean is that money can be employed as something more than a store of value that facilitates exchange. Money has a much more complicated reality for us, so complicated that not even economists nor business persons understand it, as the crisis of 'credit default swaps' and the Great Recession of 2008 demonstrates. For us, money is a financial instrument that can do things previous generations did not think it could, or should, do.

Charles Wheelan identifies 'four simple' uses for financial instruments. First, they raise capital by allowing us to borrow money; they make possible 'credit'. We borrow money we do not have today in hope and anticipation of what we will have in the future. Second, money 'stores, protects, and makes profitable use of excess capital'. The capital that is raised, even as a future possibility, can then be rented out. This occurs by establishing a 'rental rate' for capital, the rate of interest. Third, money functions as insurance against risk by futures buying. Finally, money also makes possible 'speculation' through futures buying. It can be used to insure risk or to take risk. Money buys a possible future through making credit, interest, insurance, and speculation possible. Because money is credit, interest, insurance, and speculation, it is not something 'real' to which we can point. Money is virtual. Christian ethics raises questions about several of these uses of money, especially that you should use money for futures speculation. This was traditionally condemned because it usurped God's 'time'. The future belongs only to God, and therefore to 'buy' it was to assume a god-like status. Before capitalism triumphed in the West, it had to destroy this idea, which it did.

Most of the original architects and defenders of a capitalist economy recognized it as a 'liberation' from Christianity. Once it gained ascendancy, many Christians came to defend it and see it as consistent with, if not dependent upon, Christian ideas. Others find in it the source of the secularism that pervades Western culture. The global market is even viewed as a 'simulacrum' of the Catholic Church. This is not surprising, as Adam Smith's *Wealth of Nations* received its name from Isaiah 61, a prophecy about the 'year of the Lord's favour' when Israel returns from exile. This is the same passage that Jesus quotes in his first sermon in Luke. The prophecy states:

> Strangers shall stand and feed your flocks, foreigners shall till your land and dress your vines; but you shall be called priests of the Lord....; you shall enjoy the wealth of the nations and in their riches you shall glory.
>
> (Isaiah 61:5–7)

In a biblically literate culture, many would have known the allusion in the title to Smith's revolutionary 1776 publication. Was he suggesting that if we follow his three basic principles, we would create what the prophets promised but didn't deliver? Those three principles are:

1) Everyone should act primarily based on his or her own interests.
2) No one should interfere with the market or gain an undue advantage – the playing field should be level.
3) Once these first two principles are established, then led by an 'invisible hand', the result will be social harmony.

Smith makes only one reference to the 'invisible hand' in his *Wealth of Nations*, but it is essential to his argument. Although we act self-interestedly, some force – nature, the stoic god, the logic of a free market – nonetheless works to bring about social harmony. Has this worked? Since 1776 we do not seem to have created a more harmonious world, even if we have produced great wealth.

Should Christians continue to support capitalism, or should they follow the example of liberation theologians, who seek 'liberation' from capitalism into a socialist economy? These debates, like the ones over homosexuality, have been vociferous within Christianity. They have subsided somewhat with the tearing down of the Berlin Wall in 1989. Some Christian ethics then announced the triumph of capitalism. That announcement was premature. It might also be the case that it is only within a 'Constantinian' framework that Christians think they have to determine what is the proper global economy that will work, and then try to implement it. This assumes a position of power over the culture that is quickly disappearing from Christianity, and for the better. But this does not mean that it will not offer interesting alternative economic arrangements, as it always has. Perhaps these alternative practices will become examples to the larger society, will be taken over and used for the good of all, just as has happened with hospitals and universities.

Power

Should Christians rule, and if so, how? How should they think about loyalty to the nation-state, about voting, running for and serving in political office, about crime and punishment, especially capital punishment and war? I mentioned earlier a shift that occurred from Origen and Tertullian to St Augustine; whereas the former could not countenance a 'Christian ruler', Augustine could, with qualifications. Here a key division remains among the Christian Churches. The Anabaptists, or historic peace churches, see non-violence and a refusal to rule by means of power alone, as essential to Christian faith. They tend towards a 'restitutionist' witness that privileges the first few centuries of Christianity when Christians were excluded, and excluded themselves, from the instruments of state power. The conversion of Constantine and rise of Christendom were a 'fall' from this 'original witness'.

Catholics, Orthodox, and most Protestants have traditionally rejected this position. Everyone recognizes that, on the whole, the early Christians were non-violent. We regularly find claims setting forth the ideal of peace, such as this from Origen:

> If a revolt had been the cause of the Christians existing as a separate group, the lawgiver of the Christians would not have forbidden entirely the taking of human life. He taught that it was never right for his disciples to go so far against a man, even if he should be very wicked; for he did not consider it compatible with his inspired legislation to allow the taking of human life in any form at all. Moreover, if Christians had originated from a revolt, they would not have submitted to laws that were so gentle which caused them to be killed as sheep and made then unable even to defend themselves against their persecutors.

That the early Christians tended towards non-violence is relatively uncontested; why they did so is. Some argue that the early Christians were non-violent primarily because service in the Roman military was linked to emperor-worship. Christians were less opposed to killing than idolatry. But if Origen's statement above is emblematic of early Christian opposition to violence, then it seems to have more to do with the kind of rule Jesus inaugurates than what Christians opposed. They were to embody the peaceable kingdom of the lamb who was slain, whose very body was the reconciliation of the lion and the lamb. Jesus is depicted as both. He therefore inaugurates a new kind of political rule.

Although the Anabaptists have made this 'original witness' to a different kind of political rule central to their understanding of

Christianity, we even find it in those who affirm the 'just war tradition'. For instance, Augustine opposed capital punishment against the Donatists despite that being the normal imperial method. Although he thought it appropriate to use violence to protect the innocent, he did not find it proper for a Christian to kill another in self-defence. It took some time for Christian theologians to permit killing in self-defence. Even when they did, it came with qualifications. Killing in self-defence is legitimate only as an indirect effect of a direct intention. One could not directly intend to kill merely to save one's own life. This is called the 'principle of double effect', and is very important in some Roman Catholic ethics, although what it permits is disputed. For instance, this principle suggests that in trying to protect myself, I may accidentally kill another, even though that was no part of my original intention. But some ethics, such as proportionalism, makes this the essence of ethics. Any action can have more than one effect. Some of those effects are intended, such as the intention to stop an aggression. Others are unintended, such as killing the aggressor in the attempt to stop the aggression. For this more expansive use of the principle of double effect, the unintended effects of a direct action can be legitimate even when they are not accidental but foreseen.

The just war tradition sets conditions that limit when killing is morally permissible. It was first taught by Cicero and was part of 'pagan' morality. It was reshaped within Christian tradition, and continues to undergo development. Most Christian ethicists argue that the just war tradition and Christian pacifism share a presupposition against violence, but not all. Paul Ramsey denied this claim suggesting that just war has a presupposition against disordered injustice more so than against violence. Nevertheless, the just war tradition limits legitimate reasons for which Christians can go to war and on what can be done within war. The first is called the '*jus ad bellum*' (the justice necessary to go to war) and the second the '*jus in bello*' (the justice necessary to prosecute the war). Confessors originally used these principles to determine the sinfulness of a soldier (soldiers regularly underwent penance after a war in the Middle Ages assuming they had to some extent sinned). Later they became part of international law. This transition occurred through the work of the Spanish Dominican Franciso de Vitoria (1492–1546). An important question concerning just war is raised by the contemporary Christian ethicist Dan Bell. He asks whether it should be understood primarily as a means of 'Christian discipleship' or a 'public policy checklist'. When it becomes the latter, it loses the heart of a Christian ethics even if it still does some good. The just war principles are:

Jus ad bellum (justice necessary to go to war)	*Jus in bello* (justice necessary to prosecute the war)
1. Just cause: 'protect the innocent, secure conditions necessary for human existence and basic human rights'.	1. Principle of discrimination (or non-combatant immunity): only those directly prosecuting the war can be directly intended targets.
2. Competent authority: rests on the 'prudential judgement' of those responsible for the common good.	2. Proportionality: the execution of the war must be proportionate to the purpose of the war.
3. Reasonable chance of success: war cannot produce more evil that it seeks to avoid.	
4. Right intention: the intention to enter into war cannot differ from its just cause.	
5. Last resort: all other political means to mediate conflict must be futile.	

The just war tradition is the way most Churches interpret the Fifth (or Sixth) Commandment: 'do not kill'. This tradition limited what could be done when it was in effect. It was cursorily dismissed in the modern era, but has made a comeback because of the horrors of warfare in those centuries. Even the Crusades were understood to be 'just wars', which needed the declaration of a just cause as well as the standard limitations on what could and could not be done. Of course, there have always been violations, and Anabaptist theologians often ask to what extent does this tradition actually limit war and to what extend does it justify it?

The just war tradition is no monolith; nor, for that matter, is pacifism. There are different kinds of pacifism as well; some of which represent romantic and utopian thinking that non-violence can always be an 'effective political strategy' that secures harmonious ends. Most Christian pacifists do know this is romantic. Pacifism is not primarily an effective political strategy that will always win (although we also know it does not always lose). It is primarily a witness to God's peaceable kingdom that finds in Christ the victory over the principalities and powers. This witness has even made the Roman Catholic Church revise its stand. Once it taught that pacifists were the enemies of all humankind because they seemed to be unwilling to protect innocent neighbours against unjust aggression. Now the Catholic Church recognizes that they too can serve the common good and should have a place in a just political society.

> Public authorities should make equitable provision for those who for reasons of conscience refuse to bear arms; these are nonetheless obliged to serve the human community in some other way.

(Catechism 2311)

Conclusion

So what is Christian ethics? It is the pursuit of God's goodness by people 'on the way' to a city not built by human hands. It is not a precise science but the cultivation of practical wisdom that comes from diverse sources. It draws on all that is good in God's creation and among the nations. But it also acknowledges that creatures cannot attain their true end without the gift of God's own goodness. This is no cause for despair because God communicates this goodness to us. It comes through creation, even when creatures make it unrecognizable. God nonetheless repairs creation's brokenness, first by the call of Abraham and Sarah and the creation of a unique people. They share with all of us God's gracious communication: the gift of the Divine Name, the Torah, and the Tabernacle/Temple, the dwelling-place of God on earth. God's repair of divine goodness extends to the Redemption brought by Jesus, whose life, teachings, death, resurrection, and ascension perfectly perform that goodness. He then shares it with us through his body, the Church, making possible a communication of his life through Sacraments, God's Word, and the infused virtues, gifts, fruits, and beatitudes they bring. Christian ethics is joining in God's own intentions for creation by praying the prayer he taught us: 'May your Name be holy and may your kingdom come on earth as it is in heaven.'

References

Introduction

Christopher Hitchens, *God Is Not Great: How Religion Poisons Everything* (New York: Twelve, Hatchette Book Group USA, 2007), p. 59.

Larry Hurtado, *How on Earth Did Jesus Become a God?: Historical Questions about Earliest Devotion to Jesus* (Grand Rapids, MI: William B. Eerdmans, 2005), p. 149.

Athanasius, 'On the Incarnation', in *Christology of the Later Fathers*, ed. Edward R. Hardy (Philadelphia: The Westminster Press, Library of Christian Classics, 1965), p. 105.

John Hick, *The Myth of God Incarnate* (Philadelphia: The Westminster Press, 1977), p. ix.

Sallie McFague, *The Body of God: An Ecological Theology* (Minneapolis: Fortress Press, 1993), p. 162.

David Novak, 'What to Seek and What to Avoid in Jewish-Christian Dialogue', in *Christianity in Jewish Terms*, ed. Tikva Frymer-Kensky et al. (Boulder, CO: Westview Press, 2000), p. 4.

Chapter 1: The sources of Christian ethics

Cicero, *De Officiis*, tr. Walter Miller (Cambridge, MA: Harvard University Press, 1990), p. 19 (Bk I.V).

Alasdair MacIntyre, *After Virtue* (Notre Dame, IN: University of Notre Dame Press, 1984), p. 53.

Origen, *Contra Celsum*, tr. Henry Chadwick (Cambridge: Cambridge University Press, 1980), pp. 283, 293.

Khaled Anatolios, *Athanasius: The Coherence of His Thought* (London: Routledge, 1998), p. 191.

Ambrose, 'On the Duties of the Clergy', Chapter XXIV, *Christian Classics Ethereal Library*, http://www.ccel.org/ccel/schaff/npnf210.iv.i.ii.xxiv.html accessed 2 April 2010.

James Wetzel, *Augustine and the Limits of Virtue* (Cambridge: Cambridge University Press, 1992), p. 115.

Thomas Aquinas, *Summa Theologica*, tr. Fathers of the English Dominican Province (Westminster, MD: Christian Classics, Benziger Brothers, 1981), I-II.65.2, p. 863.

Denis R. McNamara, *Letter and Spirit*, vol. 4, 'Temple and Contemplation', ed. Scott Hahn (St Paul Center for Biblical Theology, 2008), pp. 197, 199.

Margaret Barker, *The Gate of Heaven: The History and Symbolism of the Temple in Jerusalem* (London: SPCK, 1991), p. 19.

Markus Bockmuehl, *Jewish Law in Gentile Churches: Halakhah and the Beginning of Christian Public Ethics* (Grand Rapids, MI: Baker Academic, 2000), p. 159.

Pesikta Rabbati Piska 21, cited in Gerhard Lohfink, *Does God Need the Church?* (Collegeville, MN: Michael Glazier Books, 1999), p. 35.

Nancy Duff, 'Should the Ten Commandments Be Posted in the Public Realm?', in *The Ten Commandments: The Reciprocity of Faithfulness*, ed. William P. Brown (Louisville, Westminster: John Knox Press, 2004), p. 160.

Colbert Report, 14 June 2006 <http://www.colbertnation.com/the-colbert-report-videos/70730/june-14-2006/better-know-a-district—georgia-s-8th—lynn-westmoreland> accessed 2 April 2010.

Brant Pitre, *Jesus, the Tribulation and the End of Exile: Restoration Eschalogy and the Origin of the Atonement* (Grand Rapids, MI: Baker Academic, 2006), pp. 137, 143.

Robert Wilken, *The Spirit of Early Christian Thought: Seeking the Face of God* (New Haven, CT: Yale University Press, 2003), p. 273.

Thomas Aquinas, *ST* I.II 69.2.

Thomas Aquinas, *ST* I.II 68.2, rep. obj. 4.

Chapter 2: The history of Christian ethics

Wilken, *The Spirit of Early Christian Thought*, p. 29.

Yves M. J. Congar, *He is Lord and Giver of Life*, vol. II of *I Believe in the Holy Spirit* (New York: A Crossroad Herder Book, 1997), pp. 17–18, 55.

Albert Borgmann, *Technology and the Character of Contemporary Life* (Chicago: University of Chicago Press, 1987).

John Wesley, 'Sermon on the Mount IV', in *The Works of John Wesley*, ed. Albert Outler (Nashville, TN: Abingdon Press, 1984), pp. 533, 534.

Martin Luther, *Luther's Works*, vol. I, ed. and tr. Theodore Bachmann (St Louis: Concordia Publishing, 1955–86), p. 38.

Martin Luther, *Martin Luther, Selections from His Writings*, ed. John Dillenberger (New York: Anchor Books, 1961), p. 292.

Martin Luther, *Luther's Works*, vol. I, pp. 34, 36.

Gerhard O. Forde, *A More Radical Gospel* (Grand Rapids, MI: William B. Eerdmans, 2004), pp. 138, 140.

Servais Pinckaers, *The Sources of Christian Ethics* (Washington, DC: CUA Press, 1995), pp. 254, 260–5.

Pascal, *Provincial Letters*, tr. Rev. Thomas McCrie (Boston: Houghton, Osgood and Co., 1880), pp. 217–18.

K. E. Kirk, *The Vision of God: The Christian Doctrine of the Summum Bonum* (New York: Harper Torchbooks, 1931), pp. 9, 1, xvii–xviii, xxi.

Panayiotis Nellas, *Deification in Christ* (Crestwood, NY: St Vladimir's Press, 1987), pp. 38, 40.

A. N. Williams, *The Ground of Union: Deification in Aquinas and Palamas* (New York: Oxford University Press, 1999), p. 32.

John Calvin, *The Institutes of the Christian Religion*, vol. I (Philadelphia: The Westminster Press), p. 602.

Roger E. Olson, *A-Z of Evangelical Theology* (London: SCM Press, 2005), p. 173.

Raymond Brown, *The Gospel According to John XIII-XXI* (Garden City, NY: Doubleday, Anchor Bible Commentary, 1970), p. 890.

Walter M. Miller, *A Canticle for Leibowitz* (New York: Bantam Books, 1976), p. 260.

<http://www.ccel.org/ccel/schaff/anf03.iv.iii.xlii.html> accessed 2 April 2010.

St Augustine, *City of God, in The Nicene and Post-Nicene Fathers*, vol. II, ed. Philip Schaff, tr. Marcus Dods (Edinburgh: T. & T. Clark, 1979), Book. 19, chapter 17, p. 415.

David Bentley Hart, *Atheist Delusions: The Christian Revolution and Its Fashionable Enemies* (New Haven, CT: Yale University Press, 2009), pp. 195–6.

Benedict XVI's statement can be found at <http://www.bridgefolk.net/2009/04/10/pope-benedict-praises-nonviolence> accessed 2 April 2010.

Walter D. Mignolo, *The Darker Side of the Renaissance: Literacy, Territoriality and Colonization* (Ann Arbor, MI: University of Michigan Press, 2003), p. 83.

Chapter 3: Christian ethics in and beyond modernity

Norman Fiering, *Moral Philosophy at Seventeenth-Century Harvard: A Discipline in Transition* (Chapel Hill, NC: University of North Carolina Press, 1981), p. 10.

Tzvetan Todorv, *The Conquest of America* (London: Harper Perennial, 1982), p. 11.

Gustavo Gutiérez, *Las Casas: In Search of the Poor of Jesus Christ* (Maryknoll, NY: Orbis Press, 1993), p. 29.

This is Las Casas's summary of Sepúlveda's position: Bartolomé de Las Casas, *In Defense of the Indians*, tr. Stafford Poole (Dekalb, IL: Northern Illinois University Press, 1992), p. 11; see also pp. 40, 173.

Oliver O'Donovan, *Ways of Judgment* (Grand Rapids, MI: William B. Eerdmans, 2005), p. 248.

Gutiérrez, *Las Casas: In Search of the Poor of Jesus Christ*, p. 320.

Milton C. Sernett, *Afro-American Religious History: A Documentary Witness* (Durham, NC: Duke University Press, 1985), p. 177.

Maurice A. Finocchiaro, *The Galileo Affair: A Documentary History* (Berkeley, CA: University of California Press, 1989), p. 288.

Henry Kamen, *The Spanish Inquisition: A Historical Revision* (London: Weidenfeld and Nicolson, 1997), pp. 305–8.

Nietzsche, *Beyond Good and Evil* (New York: Modern Library, 1927), p. 533.

New York Times, oped, 12 March 2006.

Jürgen Habermas and Joseph Ratzinger, *The Dialectics of Secularization: On Reason and Religion* (San Francisco: Ignatius Press, 2006), p. 69.

Veritatis Splendor, in *Considering Veritatis Splendor*, ed. John Wilkins (Cleveland, OH: Pilgrim Press, 1995), p. 150.

Chapter 4: Sex, money, and power: some questions for Christian ethics

Stanley Hauerwas and William H. Willimon, *The Truth about God: The Ten Commandments in Christian Life* (Nashville, TN: Abingdon Press, 1999), p. 201.

Richard Hays, *The Moral Vision of the New Testament* (San Francisco: Harper Collins, 1996), p. 381.

David Bentley Hart, *Atheist Delusions: The Christian Revolution and Its Fashionable Enemies* (New Haven, CT: Yale University Press, 2009), p. 175.

Charles Wheelan, *Naked Economics* (New York: W. W. Norton, 2002), pp. 120–5.

Origen, *Contra Celsum*, 3.7.

Dan Bell, *Just War as Christian Discipleship: Recentering the Tradition in the Church Rather Than the State* (Grand Rapids, MI: Brazos Press, 2009).

National Conference of Catholic Bishops, *The Challenge of Peace: God's Promise and Our Response* (Washington, DC: United States Catholic Conference, 1983), p. 28.

Further reading

Introduction

For good discussions of the Christian doctrines of the Incarnation and Trinity, see, respectively, *The Incarnation: An Interdisciplinary Symposium on the Incarnation of the Son of God*, ed. Stephen T. Davis, Daniel Kendall, and Gerald O'Collins (Oxford: Oxford University Press, 2004); and *The Trinity: An Interdisciplinary Symposium on the Trinity* (Oxford: Oxford University Press, 2002). Discussions of the relationship between Christian ethics and worship are found in *The Blackwell Companion to Christian Ethics*, ed. Stanley Hauerwas and Samuel Wells (London: Wiley-Blackwell, 2010); and Bernd Wannenwetsch, *Political Worship* (Oxford: Oxford University Press, 2009). An excellent defence of Christian appropriation of the natural virtues can be found in Jennifer Herdt's *Putting on Virtue: The Legacy of Splendid Vices* (Chicago: University of Chicago Press, 2008). For a good account of the relationship between virtues and Christ's life, see Livio Melina's *Sharing in Christ's Virtues*, tr. William E. May (Washington, DC: Catholic University Press, 2001).

Chapter 1: The sources of Christian ethics

Aristotle, *Nicomachean Ethics*, tr. Martin Ostwald (Indianapolis, IN: Library of Liberal Arts, published by Bobbs-Merrill, 1985). For the limited role of natural law among the church fathers, see Robert Wilken, *The Spirit of Early Christian Thought: Seeking the Face of God* (New Haven, CT: Yale University Press, 2003), p. 321. For a discussion of the importance of the giving of the law, see Jean Louis Ska, 'Biblical

Law and the Origin of Democracy', in *The Ten Commandments*, ed.
William P. Brown (Louisville, Westminster: John Knox Press, 2004).
For the notion of Torah as a social project, see Gerhard Lohfink, *Does
God Need the Church?* (Collegeville, MN: Michael Glazier Books, 1999),
and for the Church as a 'social ethic', see Stanley Hauerwas's *Peaceable
Kingdom* (London: SCM Press, 2003). Augustine's discussion of the
beatitudes can be found in his *Commentary on the Sermon on the
Mount*, in *The Fathers of the Church Series*, and his discussion of the
gifts in *de doctrina Christiana* 2, 7: 9–11. See also Servais Pinckaers's
The Sources of Christian Ethics (Washington, DC: Catholic University
of America Press, 1995).

Chapter 2: The history of Christian ethics

Definitions of the seven deadly sins can be found in Henry Davis,
Moral and Pastoral Theology (New York: Sheed and Ward, 1952),
pp. 22–3; and in D. Stephen Long, *The Goodness of God* (Eugene,
OR: Cascade Press, 2007), pp. 166–8. For the penitentials, see John
T. McNeil and Helena M. Gamer, *Medieval Handbooks of Penance: A
Translation of the Principal Libre Poenitentiales* (New York: Columbia
University Press, 1990). For the Council of Trent, see John H. Leith,
(ed.), *Creeds of the Churches* (Atlanta: John Knox Press, 1982). For the
role of 'the lie' in Augustine, see Robert Dodaro, *Christ and the Just
Society in the Thought of Augustine* (Cambridge: Cambridge
University Press, 2004). For the relation between Church and State,
see Hugo Rahner, *Church and State in Early Christianity* (San
Francisco: Ignatius Press, 1992).

Chapter 3: Christian ethics in and beyond modernity

Jay Carter, *Race: A Theological Account* (Oxford: Oxford University
Press, 2008); William Cavanaugh, *The Myth of Religious Violence*
(Oxford: Oxford University Press, 2009); Cornel West, *Prophecy
Deliverance* (Philadelphia: The Westminster Press, 1982).

Chapter 4: Sex, money, and power: some questions for Christian ethics

For a discussion of theology and economics, see D. Stephen Long,
Divine Economy: Theology and the Market (London: Routledge,

2000). David McCarthy, *Sex and Love in the Home: A Theology of the Household* (London: SCM Press, 2004) and Brent Waters, *The Family in Christian Social and Political Thought* (Oxford: Oxford University Press, 2007) provide significant reflection on Christian ethics in relation to sex and family. For political ethics, see Oliver O'Donovan, *Desire of the Nations: Rediscovering the Roots of Political Theology* (Cambridge: Cambridge University Press, 1999) and his *The Ways of Judgment* (Grand Rapids, MI: William B. Eerdmans, 2005), as well as William Cavanaugh's *Torture and Eucharist* (London: Wiley-Blackwell, 1998). Michael Budde discusses the connections between Christianity, politics, and economics in his *The (Magic) Kingdom of God* (Boulder, CO: Westview Press, 1998). A good introduction to Christian approaches to war can be found in John Howard Yoder, *Christian Attitudes to War, Peace, and Revolution*, ed. Theodord J. Koontz and Andy Alexis-Baker (Grand Rapids, MI: Brazos Press, 2009).

Index

Abortion 98, 104, 106
Abraham 19, 23, 24, 28, 29, 37, 43, 47, 51, 70, 79, 121
Ambrose 19, 20, 74–76, 124
Anabaptist 4, 67, 68, 77, 78, 116, 117, 120
Anglican Christianity 4, 31–35, 57, 64
Aquinas, Thomas 21–23, 45, 46, 50, 59, 62, 80, 81, 112, 114, 124, 125
Ark of the Covenant 25, 36, 38–41
Aristotle 2, 13–16, 18, 23, 60, 80, 81, 84, 113, 114, 129
Artificial Contraception 107, 108
Ascension of Christ 6, 8, 121
Athanasius 9, 10, 19, 20, 123, 124
Augustine 19–21, 27, 56, 59, 66, 73, 74, 77, 81, 87, 91, 116, 118, 124, 125, 130

Babel 28, 111
Baptism 7, 51, 52, 55, 59, 67, 86, 90
Barker, Margaret 24, 124
Barth, Karl 3, 101–103, 105
Beatitudes 23, 45–50, 56, 57, 62, 65, 121, 130
Bell, Dan 119, 127
Benedict XVI (Joseph Ratzinger) 78, 103, 126

Borgmann, Albert 54, 125
Brown, John 88
Brown, Raymond 70, 125

Calvin, John 66, 88, 125
Celsus 19
Chalcedon 8
Chesterton, G. K. 53
Church 3–6, 12, 14, 23–27, 29, 36–37, 45, 52–57, 68–79, 81–83, 89, 100–102, 115, 121
Cicero 15, 19–20, 77, 118, 123
City of God 27–29, 125
Colbert, Stephen 36–7, 124
Communion 28, 29, 53, 111
Congar, Yves 53, 54, 124
Conquest 1, 70, 83–89, 126
Crusades 1, 70, 76, 83–85, 92, 98, 120
Crucifixion 4, 44, 65, 70, 102, 103
Culture 16, 24, 36, 77, 79, 86, 88, 99–102, 105, 113, 115, 116

Davidic Covenant 41, 42
Deification 60, 65, 66, 125
Diaspora (exile) 37, 38, 42–44, 115
Diognetus, Epistle to 71–73, 77
Divine Name (YHWH) 6, 23, 29, 30, 32, 35, 37, 38, 42, 46, 51–53, 98, 106, 121

Divorce 106–8
Dostoevsky, Fyodor 96–98

Economics 57, 109, 111–116, 127, 130
Election 10–12, 29, 66
Exile (see diaspora)
Exodus 29, 37, 38, 44, 52, 55, 60
Eudaimonia 2, 16
Eucharist (Lord's Supper) 7, 45, 53, 55, 58, 74, 131
Evangelical Christianity 4, 67, 88

Fall 25, 27, 65
Fetal Tissue Experimentation 110, 111
Forde, Gerhard 60, 125
Friendship 2, 10, 23, 102
Fruits (of the Spirit) 23, 45, 47, 48, 50, 121

Galileo 1, 82, 83, 89–91, 126
Gifts of Holy Spirit 23, 45–50, 56, 62, 65, 121, 130
Grace 2, 3, 51, 53, 54, 59–62, 65–67, 77, 99–102, 105
Gutiérrez, Gustavo 87, 103, 126

Habermas, Jürgen 81, 82, 103, 126
Hart, David Bentley 74, 113, 125, 127
Hauerwas, Stanley 102, 106, 127, 129
Hauser R.C. 15
Hick, John 10, 11
Hick, Edward 25, 26, 123
Hitchens, Christopher 1, 2, 11, 12, 110, 123
Hobbes, Thomas 94, 97
Holy Spirit 2, 7, 8, 23, 29, 47, 49–55, 61, 62, 99, 111
Holiness 48, 53, 74
Homosexuality 107–109, 116

Incarnation 4, 6, 8–12, 64–66, 123, 129

Inquisition 1, 70, 83, 89–93, 126
Israel 7, 12, 24, 28–30, 36, 38–44, 70, 115

Jastrow's Duck Rabbit 49
Jesus 4–13, 35, 37, 38, 40, 44–46, 61, 65, 68–70, 76, 78, 84, 86, 88, 91, 102, 115, 117, 121, 123, 124, 126, 129
John Paul II 91, 103, 104
Justice 15–21, 26, 46, 47, 57, 81, 84, 112, 118, 119
Justification, doctrine of 59–62

Kant, Immanuel 12, 80–82, 94–98,
King Jr., Martin Luther 18, 76
Kingdom of God 24–27, 37, 42, 44, 46, 48, 54, 68, 71, 117, 120, 121
Kirk, Kenneth 64, 125

Las Casa, Bartolomé de 76, 84, 85, 87, 126
Lee, Jarena 88
Liberal Protestantism 100, 101
Lord's Prayer 24, 37, 38, 53, 121
Lubac, Henri de 101–103, 105
Luther, Martin 59, 76, 125
Lutheran Christianity 31–35, 59–62

MacIntrye, Alasdair 18, 123
Marriage 106–9
Marx, Karl 93, 111
Maximus the Confessor 76, 87, 89
McFague, Sallie 11, 123
Mignolo, Walter 79, 126
Mill, John Stuart 80, 81, 104
Miller, Walter 70, 123, 125
Modernity 1, 2, 10–12, 18, 78–82, 87, 94–104, 106, 114, 120
Monarchy (Israelite) 30, 40–43, 62, 63, 77, 84, 86, 102, 103

Natural Law 3, 18–19
Nellas, Panayiotis 65, 125

Neoscholasticism 100, 101, 105
Nietzsche, Friedrich 95–99, 126
Nyssa, Gregory of 87, 89
Noahic Covenant 25–27, 58
Novak, David 12, 123

O'Donovan, Oliver 86, 87, 126, 131
Olson, Roger 67, 125
Origen 19, 72, 116, 117, 123
Orthodox Christianity 3, 4, 31–5,
   64–6, 107, 117

Pacifism 77, 88, 118, 120
Pagan Ethics 3, 13–23, 118
Pascal, Blaise 63, 125
Penance 51, 55–59, 74, 83, 107, 119
Pentecost 111
Pinckaers, Servais 62, 125, 130
Pitre, Brant 37, 124
Plato 13–15, 81
Postmodernity 94–100

Ramsey, Paul 102, 110, 118
Rawls, John 81, 82
Reformed Christianity 3, 31–35,
   45, 52, 66–67, 92, 101, 110, 121
Resurrection 6, 8, 9, 44, 52, 102
Roman Catholic Christianity 4,
   31–5, 60, 62, 63, 69, 78, 92, 100,
   107, 108, 118, 120
Rousseau, Jean Jacques 94, 96–98

Sacrament (see also Baptism and
   Eucharist) 11, 24, 44, 45, 54, 59,
   65, 66, 97, 101, 107–109, 121
Salvation (see Jesus) 54, 60, 64,
   65, 98
Sarah 23, 24, 121
Sermon on the Mount 24, 45, 46,
   91, 125, 130
Sex 26, 56, 57, 100, 106–111
Scripture 4, 6, 21, 22, 25, 27, 28,
   40, 44, 46, 48, 53, 67, 84, 90, 91,
   99, 101, 103, 108, 109, 111, 112

Ska, Jean Louis 30, 129
Slavery 1, 29, 31, 38, 52, 55, 83, 84,
   86–89, 92, 104
Smith, Adam 115, 116

Tabernacle 23, 24, 36, 39, 40,
   42, 121
Temple 23–25, 36, 41–44,
   47, 121
Ten Commandments 6, 23, 30–38,
   62, 124, 127, 130
Tertullian 13, 14, 59, 72, 73, 76,
   77, 116
Theodosius 74–76
Torah 23–25, 27, 29–39, 43–45,
   121, 130
Torture 92, 98, 104, 131
Trinity 7–8, 11, 23, 52, 129

Usury 111–113

Valladolid, debate 84, 88
Vatican II 58, 104
Vices 18, 20, 56–57, 60, 112
Virtue 2, 15–23, 45–50, 56, 57,
   60, 63–66, 73, 80–84, 102,
   104, 109, 111, 112, 121, 123,
   124, 129

War 1, 9, 10, 19, 41, 57, 73, 76,
   77, 83, 84, 87, 99, 106, 116–120,
   127, 131
Wesley, John 48, 57, 125
Wilken, Robert 45, 52, 124,
   129
Williams, A. N. 65, 66, 125
Worship 4–9, 29, 32, 35, 38,
   51–54, 64, 73, 74, 106,
   117, 129

Yoder, John Howard 77, 78,
   102, 131

Zizek, Slavoj 96–98, 126

CLASSICS
A Very Short Introduction
Mary Beard and John Henderson

This Very Short Introduction to Classics links a
haunting temple on a lonely mountainside to the glory
of ancient Greece and the grandeur of Rome, and to
Classics within modern culture – from Jefferson and
Byron to Asterix and Ben-Hur.

'The authors show us that Classics is a "modern" and
sexy subject. They succeed brilliantly in this regard …
nobody could fail to be informed and entertained – and
the accent of the book is provocative and stimulating.'

John Godwin, *Times Literary Supplement*

'Statues and slavery, temples and tragedies, museum,
marbles, and mythology – this provocative guide to the
Classics demystifies its varied subject-matter while
seducing the reader with the obvious enthusiasm and
pleasure which mark its writing.'

Edith Hall

ARCHAEOLOGY
A Very Short Introduction
Paul Bahn

This entertaining Very Short Introduction reflects the enduring popularity of archaeology – a subject which appeals as a pastime, career, and academic discipline, encompasses the whole globe, and surveys 2.5 million years. From deserts to jungles, from deep caves to mountain tops, from pebble tools to satellite photographs, from excavation to abstract theory, archaeology interacts with nearly every other discipline in its attempts to reconstruct the past.

'very lively indeed and remarkably perceptive ... a quite brilliant and level-headed look at the curious world of archaeology'

Barry Cunliffe, University of Oxford

'It is often said that well-written books are rare in archaeology, but this is a model of good writing for a general audience. The book is full of jokes, but its serious message – that archaeology can be a rich and fascinating subject – it gets across with more panache than any other book I know.'

Simon Denison, editor of *British Archaeology*

www.oup.co.uk/vsi/archaeology

INTELLIGENCE
A Very Short Introduction
Ian J. Deary

Ian J. Deary takes readers with no knowledge about the science of human intelligence to a stage where they can make informed judgements about some of the key questions about human mental activities. He discusses different types of intelligence, and what we know about how genes and the environment combine to cause these differences; he addresses their biological basis, and whether intelligence declines or increases as we grow older. He charts the discoveries that psychologists have made about how and why we vary in important aspects of our thinking powers.

'There has been no short, up to date and accurate book on the science of intelligence for many years now. This is that missing book. Deary's informal, story-telling style will engage readers, but it does not in any way compromise the scientific seriousness of the book . . . excellent.'

Linda Gottfredson, University of Delaware

'Ian Deary is a world-class leader in research on intelligence and he has written a world-class introduction to the field . . . This is a marvellous introduction to an exciting area of research.'

Robert Plomin, University of London

www.oup.co.uk/isbn/0-19-289321-1

ONLINE CATALOGUE
A Very Short Introduction

Our online catalogue is designed to make it easy to find your ideal Very Short Introduction. View the entire collection by subject area, watch author videos, read sample chapters, and download reading guides.

http://fds.oup.com/www.oup.co.uk/general/vsi/index.html

SOCIAL MEDIA
Very Short Introduction

Join our community

www.oup.com/vsi

- Join us online at the official Very Short Introductions **Facebook** page.
- Access the thoughts and musings of our authors with our online **blog**.
- Sign up for our monthly **e-newsletter** to receive information on all new titles publishing that month.
- Browse the full range of Very Short Introductions online.
- Read **extracts** from the Introductions for free.
- Visit our library of **Reading Guides**. These guides, written by our expert authors will help you to question again, why you think what you think.
- If you are a teacher or lecturer you can order inspection copies quickly and simply via our website.